Dear Educator,

Thank you for your interest in American Book Company's state-specific test preparation resources. We commend you for your interest in pursuing your students' success. Feel free to contact us with any questions about our books, software, or the ordering process.

Our Products Feature	Your Students Will Improve
Multiple-choice and open-ended diagnostic tests	Confidence and mastery of subjects
Step-by-step instruction	Concept development
Frequent practice exercises	Critical thinking
Chapter reviews	Test-taking skills
Multiple-choice practice tests	Problem-solving skills

American Book Company's writers and curriculum specialists have over 100 years of combined teaching experience, working with students from kindergarten through middle, high school, and adult education.

Our company specializes in effective test preparation books and software for high stakes graduation and grade promotion exams across the country.

How to Use This Book

Each book:

*contains a chart of standards which correlates all test questions and chapters to the state exam's standards and benchmarks as published by the state department of education. This chart is found in the front of all preview copies and in the front of all answer keys.

*begins with a full-length pretest (diagnostic test). This test not only adheres to your specific state standards, but also mirrors your state exam in weights and measures to help you assess each individual student's strengths and weaknesses.

*offers an evaluation chart. Depending on which questions the students miss, this chart points to which chapters individual students or the entire class need to review to be prepared for the exam.

*provides comprehensive review of all tested standards within the chapters. Each chapter includes engaging instruction, practice exercises, and chapter reviews to assess students' progress.

*finishes with two full-length practice tests for students to get comfortable with the exam and to assess their progress and mastery of the tested standards and benchmarks.

While we cannot <u>guarantee</u> success, our products are designed to provide students with the concept and skill development they need for the graduation test or grade promotion exam in their own state. We look forward to hearing from you soon.

Sincerely,

The American Book Company Team

PO Box 2638★Woodstock, GA 30188-1383★Phone: 1-888-264-5877★Fax: 1-866-827-3240

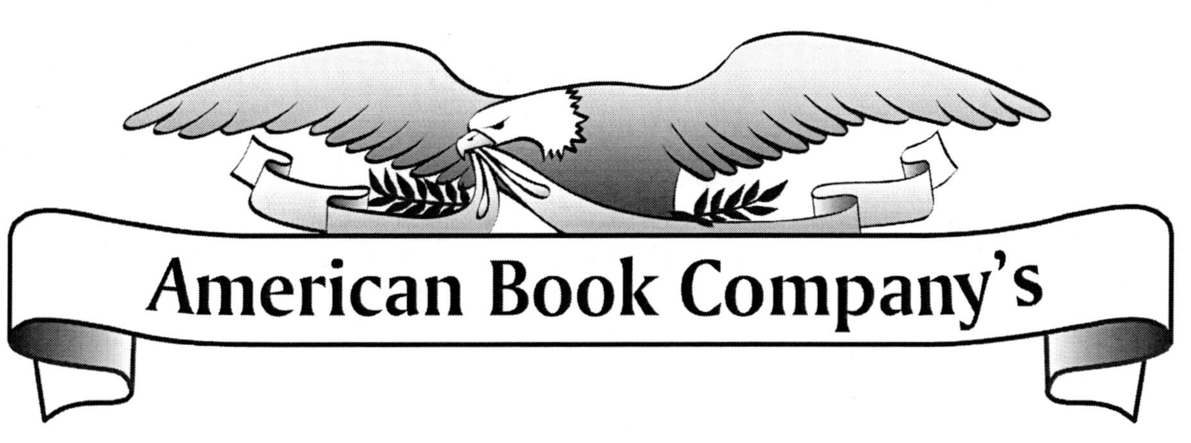

SAT WRITING

TEST PREPARATION GUIDE

WITH MULTIPLE CHOICE PRACTICE ON IMPROVING SENTENCES, IDENTIFYING SENTENCE ERRORS, AND IMPROVING PARAGRAPHS

Based on the March 2005 Revisions

Maria L. Struder
Teresa Valentine

Dr. Frank J. Pintozzi
Project Coordinator

AMERICAN BOOK COMPANY
P O BOX 2638
WOODSTOCK GEORGIA 30188-1383
Toll Free: 1 (888) 264-5877 Phone: 770-928-2834
Toll Free Fax: 1(866) 827-3240
Web site: www.americanbookcompany.com

Acknowledgements

The authors would like to gratefully acknowledge the technical contributions of Marsha Torrens.

The authors would also like to thank Mary Stoddard for her work with the graphics in this book.

A special thanks to Mike Kabel for his meticulous attention to detail in editing this book for publication.

American Book Company
PO Box 2638
Woodstock, GA 30188-1318

1st Edition November 2005

Printed in the United States of America
11/05

SAT Writing Preparation Table of Contents

PREFACE

The SAT Writing Preparation Guide will help students who are preparing to take the SAT exam.The College Board Association's expanded requirements for the SAT Writing exam are covered in this book: writing an essay and improving textual elements through multiple-choice test items. The materials in this book will also help students who want to retake the SAT Writing Test to improve a previous score. This book contains several sections: 1) general information about the book, 2) a complete writing diagnostic test, 3) an evaluation chart 4) chapters that teach the concepts and skills that improve readiness for the SAT Writing Test, and 5) two practice tests. The College Board Association writing rubrics are found in the scoring chapter of this book, allowing a precise look at student study needs. Answers to the tests and exercises are in a separate manual. The answer key also contains the appendix with additional writing prompts.

We welcome your comments and suggestions. Please contact the authors at

American Book Company
PO Box 2638
Woodstock, GA 30188-1383

Toll Free: 1 (888) 264-5877
Phone: (770) 928-2834
Fax: (770) 928-7483
web site: www.americanbookcompany.com

ABOUT THE AUTHORS

Maria L. Struder received a BA in English from Kennesaw State University (GA). She has taught writing skills at the college level and currently is enrolled in the Masters in Professional Writing Program at KSU.

Teresa Valentine is currently enrolled in the Masters of Arts in Professional Writing Program at Kennesaw State University, Kennesaw, GA. She has worked as a writing consultant coaching undergraduates from all disciplines in composition writing.

Dr. Frank J. Pintozzi is an adjunct Professor of Reading and English as a Second Language at Kennesaw State University, Kennesaw, Georgia. For over 27 years he has taught English and reading at the high school and college levels. He holds a doctorate in education from North Carolina State University in Raleigh, North Carolina. He is the author of eight textbooks on grammar, reading, writing strategies, and social studies.

TEST-TAKING TIPS

1 **Complete the chapters and practice tests in this book.** This text will help you review the skills for SAT Writing Preparation. The book also contains chapters that teach you how your essay is scored.

2 **Be prepared.** Get a good night's sleep the day before your exam. Eat a well-balanced meal that contains plenty of proteins and carbohydrates.

3 **Arrive early.** Allow yourself at least 15 – 20 minutes to find your room and get settled. Then you can relax before the exam, and you won't feel rushed.

4 **Keep your thoughts positive.** Turn negative thoughts into positive ones. Tell yourself you will do well on the exam.

5 **Practice relaxation techniques.** Some students become overly worried about exams. Before or during the test they may perspire heavily, develop an upset stomach, or have shortness of breath. If you feel any of these symptoms, talk to a close friend or see a counselor. They will suggest ways to deal with test anxiety.

Here are some quick ways to relieve test anxiety:

- Imagine yourself in your favorite place. Let yourself sit there and relax.
- Do a body scan. Tense and relax each part of your body starting with your toes and ending with your forehead.
- **The 3-12-6 method:** Inhale slowly for 3 seconds. Hold your breath for 12 seconds, and then exhale slowly for 6 seconds.

6 **Read directions carefully.** If you don't understand them, ask the proctor for further explanation before the exam starts.

7 **Answer easy questions first.** Both easy and hard questions count equally, so if you are sure about the correct answer, do the easy questions first. You'll encounter the questions at the beginning of each section, except for the Critical Reading Section.

8 **Use your best approach for answering the questions.** Some test-takers like to skim the questions and answers before reading the example. Others prefer to read the example before looking at the possible answers. Decide which approach works best for you.

9 **Choose the best answer.** Choose answers you are sure are correct. If you are not sure of an answer, take an educated guess. Eliminate choices that are definitely wrong, and choose from the remaining answers.Your score is based on the number of correct answers, not the number of questions answered.

10 **Use your answer sheet correctly.** Make sure the number of your question matches the number on your answer sheet. In this way, you will record your answers correctly. If you need to change your answer, completely erase it. Smudges or stray marks may affect the grading of your exams, particularly if they are scored by a computer. If your answers are on a computerized grading sheet, make sure the answers are dark. The scanner may skip over answers that are marked too lightly.

11 **Check your answers.** If you have the opportunity before time is called, review each section to make sure you have chosen the best responses. Change answers only if you are sure they are wrong.

SAT Writing Preparation Diagnostic Test

PART I: Essay
Time — 25 minutes

Writing the SAT essay will demonstrate your ability to express ideas and offer details. Use precise and concise language, choose a consistent, logical point of view, and organize your ideas in a logical progression with appropriate transitions.

On the actual SAT essay test, you will be given an answer sheet in which to write your essay, including a quick outline or plan. You will have no other paper on which to write.

For this practice essay, you will use your own paper. You may want to use this page to make your outline or plan, to be accustomed to the space provided for prewriting. When you write your essay, write legibly and carefully, so graders may read your work.

You have twenty-five minutes to write an essay on the writing prompt below. Write a response only to this prompt: any essay not addressing the prompt will receive a score of ZERO.

Read the following prompt and assignment carefully. Then consider your essay response.

> *Many young people do not put much thought into their own mortality. For some, youth affords the sense that one will live forever. Often, the notions of dying and growing old are of no consequence to the youthful.*
>
> Adapted from William Hazlitt's "On the Feeling of Immortality in Youth."

Assignment: What are some ways in which young people are often reckless with their mortality? Decide on your point of view, and develop it in an essay. Use reasoning and examples from your reading, studies, experience, or observations to support your position.

NOTE: There is not a word count requirement for the SAT essay. However, the essay must be long enough to demonstrate your ability to organize ideas and write them in a smooth progression. We recommend a minimum of 320 – 520 words.

Part II: 50 Multiple Choice Questions Improving Sentences, Identifying Sentence Errors, and Improving Paragraphs [Based on SAT Test Sections 3 and 10]

Time — 35 minutes

Directions: For each question, choose the best answer from among the five choices offered, circling the letter of your choice.

The following test items ask you to assess the correctness and effectiveness of written thought. In choosing responses, use the parameters set by standard written English in the areas of grammar, punctuation, sentence construction, and word choice.

In the sentences below, part of or the whole sentence is underlined. Following these sentences you will find five ways of re-phrasing the underlined part. Choice A is identical to the original; the other four responses are different. Choose the response that best expresses the meaning of the original sentence. Choose A if you think the original is correct. Choose one of the others if it is an improvement. Your choice should create the most effective sentence — clear and precise.

1. Charlotte Perkins Gilman <u>authored various works of fiction and non-fiction pieces.</u>

A. leave as is
B. authored along with various works of fiction non-fiction pieces.
C. authored various works of fiction and non-fiction.
D. authored various non-fiction pieces along with various works of fiction.
E. authored works of fiction and non-fiction variously.

2. Over the past 2,500 years, <u>about 700 versions of the popular fairy tale "Cinderella"</u> have been collected.

A. leave as is
B. about 700 versions of the popular "Cinderella" fairy tale
C. about 700 versions of "Cinderella" the popular fairy tale
D. about 700 versions of the popular fairy tale
E. the popular fairy tale "Cinderella" has about 700 versions that

3. April believes meditation is <u>important, so every day she spends time on it.</u>

A. leave as is
B. so she spends time on it each day.
C. yet she spends time on it each day.
D. so every day what she does is spend time on it.
E. so she spends time on it every day.

4. Since Ethan was nervous about making his speech, he made note cards, practiced in front of his family, and tries relaxation techniques.

A. leave as is

B. makes note cards, practices in front of his family, and tries relaxation techniques.

C. will make note cards, will practice in front of his family, and will try relaxation techniques.

D. made note cards, practiced in front of his family, and tried relaxation techniques.

E. made note cards, will practice in front of his family, and tried relaxation techniques.

5. On March 1, 1954, a 15-megaton hydrogen bomb, code-named Bravo, were exploded on the island of Bikini Atoll.

A. leave as is

B. had been exploded

C. will be exploded

D. has been exploded

E. was exploded

6. The world's largest invertebrate is the giant squid, which has been able to grow up to 70 feet long.

A. leave as is

B. which has been seen and known to grow up to 70 feet long.

C. which can grow up to 70 feet long.

D. which up to 70 feet long can grow.

E. which grows up to 70 feet long, quite large.

7. During the early 1900s, Hollywood and New Jersey were competitors for the movie industry; but by 1911 many film companies had chosen Hollywood as their home.

A. leave as is

B. movie industry, but by 1911 many film companies

C. movie industry: but by 1911 many film companies

D. movie industry but it was by 1911 that many film companies

E. movie industry. By 1911 many film companies

8. In Galveston, Texas, on June 19, 1865, Union Major General Gordon Granger announced a general order whose main purpose was to make the declaration that all slaves were free.

A. leave as is

B. that had the main purpose of declaring that all slaves were free.

C. declaring all slaves free.

D. freeing all slaves by declaring an order.

E. that made a declaration.

9. The "eye," or center, of a hurricane is relatively calm and is encircled by powerful winds and storms.

A. leave as is

B. The "eye" is the center of a hurricane

C. The center of a hurricane is the "eye" and

D. The "eye" or center of a hurricane

E. A hurricane's center "eye" and

10. Annie had hoped to get the main character's part in the play, but she seemed happy for and willing to give support of Diane.

A. leave as is

B. she seemed happy for and supportive of Diane.

C. she seemed to be happy for and to be supportive of Diane.

D. she seemed to have happiness and support for Diane.

E. she seems to have been happy for and supportive of Diane.

11. Citizens of the United States have many rights, one of which happens to be free speech that allows public protest.

A. leave as is

B. rights, public protest is allowed by one and that's free speech.

C. rights, for example is free speech, allows public protest.

D. rights, like free speech, which allows public protest.

E. and one of the rights is free speech, and that allows public protest.

> The next group of test items evaluates your skill in recognizing and correcting grammar and usage errors. There is either one error or no error in each of the test items; none of the items has more than one error. If there is an error, it is underlined and labeled with a letter A through E. If there is an error in the test item, choose the one underlined part you would need to change to correct the test item. If there is no error and the test item is correct as is, select choice E. In choosing responses, use the parameters of standard written English.

12. The earliest river valley civilization is believed (A) to have been Mesopotamia, which (B) is locates (C) in present day Iraq in an area that is called (D) The Fertile Crescent. No Error (E)

13. During (A) the Watergate Scandal, President Nixon resigned (B) because the House Judiciary committee was fixing (C) to impeach (D) him. No Error (E)

14. The Hadrosaur, one of the ornithopodan dinosaurs, had (A) teeth arranged (B) like many other mammals; the upper and lower teeth worked (C) together to grind there (D) food. No Error (E)

15. The Fair Pay Act, as introduced in 1999, amends (A) the Fair Standards Act of 1938 by prohibiting (B) discrimination in the payment of wages accounting (C) to gender, race, or (D) national origin. No Error (E)

16. Geronimo, the most famous (A) of the Apaches, is remembered as a remarkable (B) leader because of his sharp (C) intelligence and his fearlessly (D) in battle. No Error (E)

17. Kudzu, a vine with lush green leaves and
A
beautiful purple flowers, first appeared in the
B
U.S. at the 1876 Centennial Exposition in
Philadelphia and became popular in the
C
1930's when soil conservationists urge farm-
D
ers to plant it to halt erosion. No Error
E

18. During the terrible Irish famine of 1847–
A
1852, large numbers of Irish people
B C
immigrate to the United States. No Error
D E

19. During the 1880's and 1890's, Andrew Carn-
A
egie was a prominent leader of the steel
B
industry and one of the rich men in the
C
world. No Error
D E

20. Booker T. Washington was a great leader for
him people by encouraging
A B
them to learn skills to become economically
C
equal with the white race. No Error
D E

21. For centuries, the southern giant petrel, a
A
large, long-living bird, was reviled as a
B C
bird full of disgusting habits. No Error
D E

22. The Heimlich maneuver is an emergency
A
technique for preventing suffocating when a
B C
person's windpipe becomes blocked by an
D
object or a piece of food. No Error
E

23. Both the students who decided to run for
A B
treasurer is good candidates. No Error
C D E

24. Michael likes to tell stories about
A B
when him and his mother took a trip to
C D
Mexico. No Error
E

25. Mrs. Winslow has a habit to changing the
A B
décor of her home at least twice a year to
C
reflect her various moods. No Error
D E

26. The Catawba were a great and powerful
A B
tribe of Native Americans who lived in what is now
C
the states of North and South Caro-
D
lina. No Error
E

27. Marissa decided to write a letter to the editor
A B
of the paper about an article she considered
C
to be inappropriate. No Error
D E

28. The friendship between (A) Max and Katie are (B) especially close; they (C) considered one another (D) family. No Error (E)

29. The amount (A) of poverty in a country has little (B) to do with its (C) population density or even its supply (D) of resources. No Error (E)

Directions: The passage below is an early draft of an essay. There are revisions which need to be made in the essay.

Read over the passage noting the flow of the paragraphs and the sense of the sentences. Then read the following questions and choose the best response for each. The questions cover several elements of the writing process: improving sentence structure or word choice, organization, point of view, and paragraph development. In choosing responses, use the parameters set by standard written English.

Questions 30 – 35 refer to the passage below.

(1) My best friend Katie dreams of being a counselor because of what she is best at. **(2)**Listening to people. **(3)**I never hesitate to talk to Katie when I'm in need of advice. **(4)**My problems she is usually able to solve after listening to me talk. **(5)**Others appreciate Katie's ability to listen and give advice. **(6)**She is always willing to take the time to help anyone with his or her problems. **(7)**Because of this, Katie has a reputation at our school for being a good listener.

(8) On one occasion, I was very upset about having made a bad grade on a test I had studied quite hard for. **(9)**I immediately sought out Katie to talk to, knowing that she would be able to make me feel better. **(10)**It seems like there is always someone who wants to talk to Katie about something. **(11)**After she helped me sort out my problems, I felt much better. **(12)**I was able to look to the future instead of dwelling on the past.

(13) Katie is truly an amazing person. **(14)**Her ability to listen and give sound advice makes her a wonderful friend to have. **(15)**However, she deserves the good reputation she has among her peers, and she will no doubt make a wonderful counselor one day. **(16)**I feel privileged to have Katie as my best friend and know that she deserves all the good things that will certainly come her way.

30. Which of the following is the best way to revise and combine sentences 1 and 2? (reproduced below)

My best friend Katie dreams of being a counselor because of what she is best at. Listening to people.

A. Because of listening to people, what my best friend Katie is best at, she dreams of being a counselor.

B. My best friend Katie dreams of being a counselor because of what she is best at and that is listening to people.

C. My best friend Katie, who dreams of being a counselor because of what she is best at, listening to people.

D. My best friend Katie dreams of being a counselor because of what she is best at: which is listening to people.

E. Listening to people is what my best friend Katie is best at, and because of that she dreams of being a counselor.

31. Which of the following is the best way to revise sentence 4? (reproduced below)

My problems she is usually able to solve after listening to me talk.

A. best as is

B. She is usually able to solve my problems after listening to me talk.

C. After listening to me talk, my problems she is usually able to solve.

D. My problems, after listening to me talk, she is usually able to solve.

E. She is usually able to solve, after listening to me talk, my problems.

32. Which of the following best replaces *because of this* in sentence 7?

A. Consequently

B. However

C. Whatever

D. To my surprise

E. Despite this

33. Which of the following sentences should be removed from the second paragraph to improve its unity?

A. sentence 8

B. sentence 9

C. sentence 10

D. sentence 11

E. sentence 12

34. Which of the following is the best way to revise the underlined portion of sentence 15? (reproduced below)

However, she deserves the good reputation she has among her peers, and she will no doubt make a wonderful counselor one day.

A. best as is

B. however

C. coincidentally

D. perhaps

E. doubtfully

35. What strategy does the writer employ in the third paragraph?

A. exaggeration

B. argue in a cynical tone

C. deviate from the main topic

D. spread rumors

E. repeat words

36. From as early as the 1920's, regular moviegoers millions of Americans have been.

A. regular moviegoers millions of Americans have been.

B. millions of Americans have regularly been known as moviegoers.

C. millions of Americans have been regular moviegoers.

D. americans have been regular moviegoers in millions.

E. americans, millions of them, have been regular moviegoers.

37. Since the late nineteenth century, researchers from the United States and Russia have recorded an eleven percent reduction in the total volume of ice in the world's smaller glaciers.

A. leave as is

B. in the volume of ice in the glaciers of the world that are smaller.

C. in the volume of ice in the world's smallest glaciers, in total.

D. in the volume of ice, in total, in the world's smallest glaciers.

E. in the smaller glaciers of the world, in total volume of ice

38. Approximately one out of fourteen teenagers, for a sports injury, has required hospitalization.

A. leave as is

B. has required hospitalization for a sports injury.

C. has required, for a sports injury, hospitalization.

D. have been required to have had hospitalization for a sports injury.

E. requiring hospitalization for a sports injury.

39. The northern lights, more formally known as the aurora borealis, usually occur around the earth's magnetic poles in a range of 1,200 miles.

A. leave as is

B. in a range of 1,200 miles, around the earth's poles, usually occur.

C. usually occur in a range, around 1,200 miles, around the earth's magnetic poles.

D. usually occur in a range of 1,200 miles from the earth's magnetic poles.

E. 1,200 miles, or in that range from the earth's magnetic poles, usually occur.

40. Mariah and her family are excited about their traveling to Europe this summer.

A. leave as is

B. over their traveling

C. about traveling

D. about going to travel

E. about being going to travel

41. An annual survey by the National Center on Addictions and Substance Abuse at Columbia University in New York revealed that serious drug abuse is common in those who are teenagers and who are not emotionally close and secure with their fathers.

A. leave as is

B. those teenagers

C. in teenagers

D. in those teenagers

E. in teenagers who are those

42. Some words are homographs: spelled alike but with different origins and meanings.

A. leave as is

B. different origins and meanings they have, but are spelled alike.

C. different origins and meanings are all that keep them from being spelled alike.

D. they are spelled alike but have different origins and meanings.

E. origins and meanings are different, but they are spelled alike.

43. Young people, when beginning to make a decision about which college to attend, there are many factors to consider.

A. leave as is

B. When young people are beginning to attend college and make a decision about which one

C. When a young person begins to make a decision about which college to attend,

D. When it becomes time for a young person to attend college, they must begin to decide.

E. When beginning to make a decision about which college to attend, young people,

44. Primary resources include speeches, letters, diaries, and also journals.

A. leave as is

B. includes speeches, letters, diaries, and journals.

C. are those resources which include speeches, letters, diaries, and also journals.

D. include speeches, letters, diaries, and also including journals.

E. include speeches, letters, diaries, and journals.

45. Columbus' successful voyage in 1492 happened to prompt a papal bull that divided the globe between rivals Spain and Portugal.

A. leave as is

B. prompted a papal bull that divided the globe between rivals Spain and Portugal.

C. divided the globe between rivals Spain and Portugal because of a papal bull that was prompted.

D. was prompted by a papal bull that happened to divide between the globe rivals Spain and Portugal.

E. prompted a papal bull that between the globe divided rivals Spain and Portugal.

46. Mauna Kia, which means "white mountain" in the Hawaiian language, is the tallest mountain in Hawaii.

A. leave as is

B. which in the Hawaiian language means "white mountain"

C. which means, in the Hawaiian language, "white mountain"

D. in the Hawaiian language which means "white mountain"

E. "white mountain" is what that means in the Hawaiian language

47. It is amazing how the Japanese have retained their cultural heritage while at the same time managing to simultaneously integrate many parts of Western culture.

A. leave as is

B. while managing to simultaneously integrate many parts of Western culture at the same time.

C. while simultaneously integrating many parts of Western culture.

D. while integrating, simultaneously, many parts of Western culture.

E. while many parts of Western culture are being integrated into the Japanese culture simultaneously.

48. Stuart Parkins of the World Wide Fund for Nature says that demand for the exotic pelts of giant pandas are strongest in Taiwan but exists also in Japan and Hong Kong.

A. leave as is

B. in Taiwan is strongest but that it also exists in Japan and Hong Kong.

C. exists in Japan and Hong Kong but are strongest in Taiwan.

D. is strongest in Taiwan but exists also in Japan and Hong Kong.

E. in Taiwan exists the strongest but also exists in Japan and Hong Kong.

49. The hoatzin is a type of bird who grinds up the leaves it eats in a specialized muscular crop.

A. leave as is

B. that has a specialized muscular crop that, after eating leaves, grinds them up.

C. that eats leaves by grinding them up in a specialized muscular crop.

D. that, in a specialized muscular crop, grinds up what it eats, leaves.

E. who eats leaves and in a specialized muscular crop grinds them up.

50. Antarctica would be the smallest continent if you counted only the actual land, but its ice covering makes it larger than Europe or Australia.

A. leave as is

B. Counting the actual land only, Antarctica would be the smallest continent

C. The smallest continent is what Antarctica would be if you counted only actual land

D. Counting only actual land would make Antarctica to be the smallest continent

E. Antarctica's actual land, if you counted it only, would be the smallest continent

Evaluation Chart - Diagnostic Test

On the following chart, circle the question numbers that you answered incorrectly and evaluate the results. Then turn to the appropriate topics (listed by chapters), read the explanations, and complete the exercises. Review the other chapters as needed. Finally, complete the **SAT Writing Preparation Practice Tests** to further prepare yourself for the SAT Writing Test.

NOTE: Some questions may appear under multiple chapters because those questions require multiple skills.

Chapter Reference	Pages	Question Number
Chapter 1: Writing Paragraphs	13 – 31	30, 33, 35
Chapter 2: Appropriate Vocabulary and Point of View	33 – 44	10,13, 15, 16, 26, 50
Chapter 3: Critical Thinking	45 – 46	35
Chapter 4: Writing the Opinion Essay	57 – 74	
Chapter 5: Using the Write Stuff: Avoiding Errors	75 – 94	3, 7, 9, 21, 22, 29, 42, 43
Chapter 6: Improving Sentences, the SAT Way	95 – 114	1, 2, 10, 11, 14, 19, 20, 24, 25, 27, 29, 31, 32, 36, 37, 38, 39, 41, 46, 47
Chapter 7: Improving Paragraphs	115 – 132	12, 30, 31, 32, 333, 4, 40, 48, 49
Chapter 8: Editing the Essay	133 – 148	2, 5, 6, 11, 12, 13, 17, 18, 19, 23, 26, 28, 29, 34, 35, 36
Chapter 9: Neophyte's Guide to Scoring SAT Essays	149 – 162	

Writing Evaluation Chart for Diagnostic and Practice Tests

The chapters in this book will provide you with opportunities to write essays. You will find several writing prompts in the appendix for writing practice.

Keep your compositions in one folder. As you practice writing, use the Writing Evaluation Chart below to track your progress.

For each essay, work with your instructor/tutor to assign a grade in each category. If you have an excellent grasp of the skill, write **E** for **Excellent**. If you use the skill well enough to pass, write **P** for **Passing**. If you need more practice, write **NP** for **Needs Practice**. The number listed next to each skill indicates the chapters which discuss that skill. Read and review the chapters you need to improve each concept and skill.

Writing Skills	Chapter Number	Diagnostic Test	Practice Test 1	Practice Test 2
Writes Clear Topic Sentences	1			
Effective Supporting Details	1			
Maintains Consistent Tone	2			
Careful Reading and Critical Thinking	3			
Transitions and Coherence	7, 8			
Effective Word Choice	5, 6			
Sentence Variety	5			
Clear and Concise Words or Ideas	3, 4, 8			
Grammar and Punctuation	5, 6			
Proofreding and Editing	8			

Chapter 1
Writing Paragraphs

Just as the quality of a building depends on the materials used in its construction, the quality of an essay is only as effective as the **paragraphs** that comprise it. When faced with the assignment of writing a well organized, cohesive SAT essay in 25 minutes, you will develop the essay one paragraph at a time. In this chapter, we will practice composing paragraphs, the building blocks of a good essay.

The purpose of paragraphs is to organize ideas. In chapter 4 of this book, you will learn about the "quick and messy" outline, in which you jot down ideas that come to mind when you read the writing prompt. But after you write several notes, what is the next step? You immediately organize them, grouping them into sentences and paragraphs.

In chapter 4, you will also learn about the three kinds of paragraphs: introduction, body, and conclusion. For now, we will look at the basic features that constitute all effective paragraphs. This chapter discusses the following elements of paragraph writing.

- **Paragraph Structure**
- **Writing Clear Topic Sentences**
- **Writing Effective Supporting Sentences**
- **Writing Strong Concluding Sentences**
- **Organizing Paragraphs**
- **Using Convincing Language**

Paragraph Structure

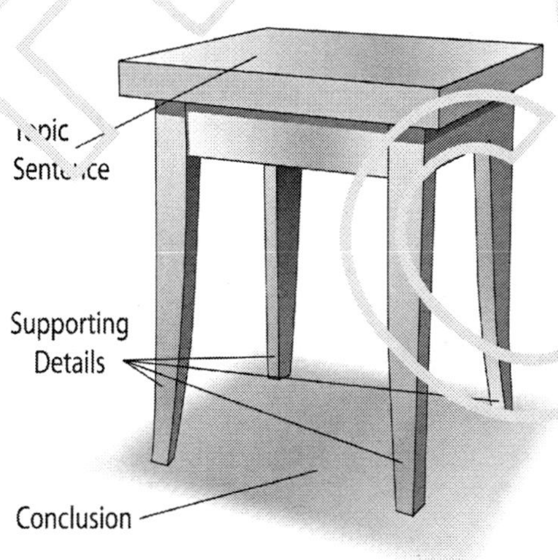

An easy way to understand the **structure** of a paragraph is to compare it to a table. The topic sentence is like the table top. Just as the table top's purpose is to provide a flat surface for writing or eating, the **topic sentence**'s purpose is to give the reader a broad view. Without legs, the table top will not stand, so the topic sentence needs **details**, examples, and personal observations to support it. Finally, a table that rocks on an uneven floor is not reliable. In the same way, a paragraph that rests on an unclear or irrelevant **conclusion** will appear unstable.

For the purposes of the SAT essay, a paragraph may contain 4 to 6 sentences. These sentences consist of three types:

- **A topic sentence**, which states the main idea
- **Supporting sentences,** which support the main idea
- **A concluding sentence,** which ties the paragraph into the main idea

Here's an example which illustrates the three types of sentences and their functions. The paragraph is part of an essay written in response to the following sample SAT prompt:

Sample Prompt

> Think carefully about the issue described in the excerpt below and about the assignment that follows it.
>
> *According to Franklin D. Roosevelt, "Democracy cannot succeed unless those who express their choice are prepared to choose wisely. The real safeguard of democracy, therefore, is education."*
>
> **Assignment**: What is your opinion about the claim that an uneducated society cannot produce a true democracy? Plan and write an essay in which you develop your point of view (opinion) on the issue. Support your point of view with reasons and evidence brought from your own experience, your studies, or from your observations.

Sample Paragraph

Topic sentence	(1) One example of how a lack of education supports tyranny can be found in the history of our own country.
Supporting sentences	**(2)** American slave owners of the 18th and 19th centuries made it illegal for slaves to learn to read or write. **(3)** They knew that literacy and knowledge would cause slaves to want freedom and control over their own lives. **(4)** Frederick Douglass was born in slavery but became a famous writer and abolitionist after teaching himself to read and write. **(5)** An education made it possible for him to learn about the world around him, evaluate it, and decide how to improve it.
Concluding sentence	**(6)** This is the core of democracy.

Each sentence in the above paragraph contributes to the coherence of the paragraph in the following ways:

Sentence 1: Topic Sentence. The writer introduces the main idea.

Sentence 2: The writer narrows the topic's focus. The topic goes from the broad idea of our national history to a specific chapter: slavery.

Sentence 3: The 3rd sentence develops the connection between the lack of democracy (tyranny) and the lack of education.

Sentence 4: The 4th sentence gives a specific example of an individual in history who personified the power of education.

Sentence 5: The 5th sentence shows how education empowered Douglass to make informed choices.

Sentence 6: The 6th sentence, or concluding sentence, establishes the connection between the empowerment of education, described in sentence 5, and democracy, the topic.

Now we will look more closely at ways of writing each type of sentence in a paragraph.

WRITING CLEAR TOPIC SENTENCES

The previous section shows that you can organize a paragraph around a single idea, stated in the **topic sentence**. The topic sentence imparts two important pieces of information. It tells

- the subject of the paragraph and
- what you want the reader to know about the subject.

To write a topic sentence, begin by asking yourself:

1. What is the subject of the paragraph?
2. What do I want the reader to know?

Then use the answers to these questions to form a topic sentence. For example:

Subject of the paragraph	What you want the reader to know	Topic sentence
New democracy in Afghanistan	Schools reopened when democracy started.	The new democracy in Afghanistan gives us an example of how education is necessary for democracy.

Think of the topic sentence as your compass when you write, helping to stay focused on your essay's position. If you feel yourself getting lost or losing direction in the body paragraphs, refer back to the topic sentence to reorient yourself. If a sentence doesn't fit in some way to the topic or you feel it's repeating information already stated, delete it from your essay.

TIP

The topic sentence states what you want the reader to know about the subject of the paragraph.

STATING A SINGLE IDEA IN BROAD TERMS

Writing a topic sentence can be easy, but writing a *good* topic sentence gets a little more challenging. Remember, a paragraph discusses a single idea, so an effective topic sentence presents only a single idea. Keep in mind the metaphor of a paragraph as a table. The tabletop needs to be broad enough to cover all the ideas that support it, so you should state a **single topic** in broad, general terms. Look at the following examples.

Single Idea

***Limited*: Multiple Ideas**	***Improved*: Single Idea**
Without the education of women and ethnic minorities, a democracy is not complete.	Without the education of minorities, a democracy is not complete.
Education ensures freedom of choice and social equality to the citizens of a democracy.	Education ensures social equality for the citizens of a democracy. OR Education ensures informed choices for the citizens of a democracy.
An education, with financial independence, enables citizens of a democracy to be more active in their society.	An education allows citizens to take a more active part in their society. OR Financial independence enables citizens of a democracy to be more active in their society.

Broad Statement

***Limited*: Narrow Statement**	***Improved*: Broad Statement**
I contacted my state representative after reading about the medicare cutbacks that would affect my grandparents.	My ability to read and write has prompted me to take advantage of my rights as a citizen in a democratic country
In Ray Bradbury's *Farenheit 451*, books are considered an enemy of the state	Literature contains several examples of societies which oppress people by repressing education.
I did not appreciate the value of living in a democracy until I studied the birth of my country.	Education teaches people about the value of democracy itself.

Remember: A good topic sentence presents a single topic in broad, general terms.

Practice 1: Writing Clear Topic Sentences

The following topic sentences are either too narrow in focus or contain more than one idea. On a separate sheet of paper, rewrite each into a clear topic sentence.

1. Two of the most common forms of government control are high taxes and mandatory education.
2. Snowmobiles and powerboats infringe on the rights of Americans to enjoy their national wilderness parks.
3. Many zoo animals spend their days restlessly pacing an area smaller than most teen's bedrooms.
4. If I want to take a chance with my safety and not wear a bike helmet, that should be my right.
5. Public schools should provide students with personal laptops and technology training to prepare us for jobs in the future.

WRITING EFFECTIVE SUPPORTING SENTENCES

Your topic sentence, which presents a single idea in general terms, is like the opening of the door. It leads to a more specific argument of that idea. The supporting sentences of a paragraph take the general idea and clarify it with specific details. When writing the SAT essay, you are encouraged to support your ideas by using:

- examples from literature, history, and other studies
- personal experience and observations
- logical reasoning.

A topic sentence presents your idea to the reader. It is up to you to back up your idea by providing clear, logical support. **Supporting details** are specific statements that expand on the main idea but do not *restate* the main idea.

To illustrate how to write supporting details, we will look at some possible responses to the following SAT prompt:

> Think carefully about the issue in the quotations and the assignment below.
>
> 1. *Land: A part of the earth's surface, considered as property. The theory that land is property subject to private ownership and control is the foundation of modern society, and is eminently worthy of the superstructure.* –Ambrose Bierce
> 2. *So great moreover is the regard of the law for private property, that it will not authorize the least violation of it; no, not even for the general good of the whole community.* –William Blackstone
>
> **Assignment**: Does an individual's right to the use of his or her property have priority over the general good of society? Plan and write an essay in which you develop your point of view on the issue. Support your opinion with reasons and evidence brought from your own experience and studies.

1. **Supporting details are more than restatements of the topic sentence.** Supporting details provide reasons and examples that show why the main idea is true. Look at the following example. The topic sentence of the paragraph is underlined.

***Limited*: Restates Topic**	***Improved*: Provides Example**
When individuals buy property, they have rights over the use of that property. When you buy property, you own it. It belongs to you. Therefore, you have the right to do what you want with that property. Property rights mean that if you own property, you have rights over its use. Others cannot dictate how you use your own property, because it belongs to you.	When individuals buy property, they have rights over the use of that property. For example, if a homeowner decided to dam a stream on her property in order to create a small lake, she has the right to do so. Neighbors or governments should not be able to tell her how to landscape her own property. This would be a denial of her basic freedom of expression and her right to happiness.

2. **Supporting details are related to the topic.** If the details digress from the topic, these unrelated ideas can weaken the strength of the paragraph, confusing the reader.

***Limited*: Unrelated**	***Improved*: Related**
In many instances, property ownership rights interfere with the greater good of society. I know of a home owner in a rural area who decided to raise fighting roosters in his barn. Most of the neighbors objected because they felt rooster fighting was unethical. These fights often end in the death of one of the fighting roosters. People felt that the neighbor was practicing animal cruelty and that animals have a right to life too. No one should have a right to play sports that are cruel to animals.	In many instances, property ownership rights interfere with the greater good of society. I used to visit the farm of a friend whose neighbor decided to raise fighting roosters. The noise and the smell were sometimes unbearable. The neighbors also worried about the health hazards of the rooster farm's waste material, which flowed into a creek they all shared. In this situation, the rights of the neighbors to peace, quiet, and health were denied by one property owner exercising his rights.

3. **Supporting details are specific examples, not general statements.** The topic sentence is a general statement, but you should explain it in detail. Be as specific as you can.

***Limited*: General**	***Improved*: Specific**
<u>Property rights actually support the general good of society</u>. Having the right to own property makes people free. If people could not have rights over their own property and belongings, they would be no better than slaves in a world that they had no control over. When people have control over their own world, they are happier. When individuals have property rights, they contribute to a happier society.	<u>Property rights actually support the general good of society</u>. One can see this clearly by considering the case of the American Indians who were forcibly removed from the land they considered home. Although they did not think in terms of ownership of the earth, they had the right to live where they could survive. If settlers had allowed them their rights to keep what they felt was their home, that chapter of history may have been one of mutual benefit and peace, rather than a tragedy of mass deaths and exile.

> Remember: Supporting details are specific statements that are related to the topic of the paragraph. They do not just restate the main idea.

Practice 2: Supporting Your Main Idea

Read each group of sentences below. If the group forms a well-developed paragraph, write "Correct" in the space provided. If the group restates the topic sentence, contains unrelated ideas, or uses general statements instead of specifics, state the problem, and rewrite the paragraph on a separate sheet of paper.

1. Property rights need to be curbed by laws that protect the common good. If society does not have laws that protect all citizens' rights, then the rights of certain people effectively deprive others of their rights. Laws are needed to protect society as a whole against the misuse of rights by a few. Therefore, if a property owner abides by the general laws of the land protecting others' rights, then that property owner should be able to practice his own rights without hurting others.

____

2. Sometimes the rights of an individual affect the rights of society as a whole. For instance, people have a right to listen to whatever music they like, as loud as they want. But some people play music in their cars so loudly that they become a hazard on the road. If an ambulance approaches them from behind, these people will not hear the siren. If they are not looking in their mirror, they will continue driving instead of pulling over. This may cause the ambulance a delay in getting to its destination, endangering someone's life. People who play extremely loud music in their cars pose a problem to the other drivers on the road.

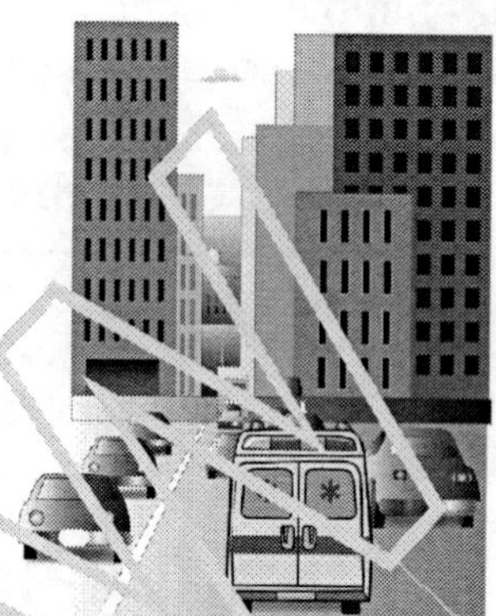

3. People have a right to own property and to use it as they choose to. The basic principles of our country are based on personal freedom. No one has the right to take another person's freedom away. No one has the right to tell another person how to live or what to do with his property. There is no freedom without the freedom of self determination. In order to have self determination, human beings must have the right to own property and to live as they wish. The right to property ownership and self determination are essential to the good of society.

WRITING STRONG CONCLUDING SENTENCES

Each paragraph expands on a specific idea that illustrates the main point, or *thesis*, of your paper. The word thesis comes from the Greek word for to put, and you may think of a thesis as the statement that puts forward an idea or argument, like a king upon a throne. Without details and examples, however, the statement dangles, nervous and unsure. As the supporting details develop and take root in your paragraph, the thesis becomes strengthened, like a king beloved by his subjects. And just as villagers swore loyalty to their king, paragraphs have to align themselves with their thesis to maintain unity in your writing.

The concluding sentence of a paragraph:

- Summarizes the topic and details of the paragraph.
- Ties the topic of the paragraph into the main idea, or thesis, of the essay.

The best way to write a concluding sentence is to glance over your introductory paragraph and ask, "How does this paragraph relate to my essay's main idea?" Then write a sentence that addresses that question.

Look at the following examples of paragraphs with concluding sentences that tie into the main idea of the essay. Notice how the concluding sentence brings the reader back to the main idea of the essay.

Main Idea of Essay	Paragraph with Concluding Sentence
Happiness comes from within us, not from circumstances around us.	Many heroes and leaders have given us examples of how happiness can exist regardless of circumstances. Mother Theresa of Calcutta, for example, lived amid the most difficult conditions imaginable. But it is rare to find a picture of her not smiling or looking peaceful – even joyful. She seemed to contain a great reservoir of happiness within her, which even the wealthiest people on earth might envy. Perhaps her happiness came from her faith and her choice to help, rather than to avoid difficulties. In any case, it obviously came from within her, and not from the impoverished and tragic circumstances that surrounded her.
Arts and literature are still as valuable to society as technology is.	One way to illustrate the value of arts and literature in society is to look at a literary example of a society without arts or literature. Lois Lowry's *The Giver* depicts a world in which technology and human ingenuity have eliminated suffering, illness, and pain. But they have also eliminated all the materials that inform art and literature: the wonder of life, of suffering, and of beauty. From this world, the main character, Jonas, risks his life to escape. This is an extreme example, but points starkly to the need for a balance in life, in which arts and literature are valued as much as technology is.
I believe, along with Asimov, that people who use violence to solve problems do so because of a lack of competence in alternative methods.	Often people use violence simply because they are incompetent in communicating their needs. Most of us have observed young children who have not yet mastered speech. It is not uncharacteristic of them to bat, kick, grab, and push their playmates down, merely to gain access to a toy. This behavior is usually met with an equal volley of pounding, kicking, and screaming, as each child inarticulately and violently expresses his or her frustration. If nature had endowed young children with the skills of speech, cooperation, and willingness to compromise, all the flailing would be unnecessary. The same principle of the lack of peace skills can be applied to violence between adults.

Practice 3: Writing Strong Concluding Sentences

Chose a sample SAT topic from Appendix A. Write one paragraph in response to the topic. Underline your concluding sentence. Review it yourself and see that it ties the main idea of the paragraph into the main idea of the essay. Then exchange your paragraph with another student and discuss each other's concluding sentences.

ORGANIZING PARAGRAPHS

Now that you have a topic sentence and good ideas for supporting details, you must decide how you want to organize your paragraph. A paragraph is not put together haphazardly, but has structure and organization. For the purposes of the SAT essay, this chapter will discuss the organizational patterns of **cause and effect**, **comparing and contrasting ideas**, and **statement and support**.

The paragraphs in this section are taken from sample essays that respond to the following writing assignment:

> Think carefully about the issue and the assignment below.
>
> 1. Television viewers and networks contend that millions of people, including children, watch violent television every day and do not become violent.
> 2. On the other hand, psychologists have claimed that from regularly watching violence on television, young people can become less sensitive to the suffering of others. They develop a more mistrusting attitude towards their world and are more likely to use aggression towards others.
>
> **Assignment**: Do you think that violent content on television affects people's behavior? Plan and write an essay in which you develop your point of view (opinion) on the issue. Support your opinion with reasons and evidence brought from your own experience, your studies, or your observations.

CAUSE AND EFFECT

Showing a direct link, or **cause and effect** relationship, between observed events and the factors that led to them can make your point with power and directness. This method is especially useful with prompts such as the one above, which asks about the effects of a given cause.

The following paragraph uses **cause and effect** to show how television violence results in certain behavior in children.

Statistics and nationwide studies can say all they want about television violence and behavior, but most of us have witnessed it firsthand in children. I often babysit a family of three young children on weekends and evenings, watching them play high-spirited, active games. But when they are allowed to watch television at night, they almost always have difficulty going to bed afterwards. As soon as the television is turned off, they begin their copycat games

> of good guys and bad guys. This play almost always involves battles or fights of some kind. After they watched *The Lord of the Rings*, they played Orcs and Hobbits for days afterwards, using sticks for swords and pretending to kill or be killed. The effect of the violent elements of this movie on these children was immediate and unequivocal.

In the above paragraph, the writer draws a direct link from personal experience between the behavior of children (effect) and the content of television shows (cause).

Comparing and Contrasting Ideas

Ideas can be powerfully illustrated by **comparing** or **contrasting** them with other ideas.

In the following paragraph, the writer compares the effect of violent television on children with the effect of secondary cigarette smoke on children:

> To say that television violence does not affect children because many people watch it without becoming criminals is like saying that secondary cigarette smoke does not affect children because many people are exposed to it and do not become sick. How can we measure the effects on all children? Thousands of children with tendencies towards respiratory weakness develop asthma when exposed to secondary smoke on a regular basis. Other children may not, but they may develop severe allergy problems later in life. In the same way, children exposed to violent content in television will react to it differently. Some may be affected in ways that do not show up until later in life. I believe that if material has the potential of harming those who are exposed to it, whether it is cigarette smoke or violent television, we should be cautious in exposing children to that material.

The following paragraph **contrasts** two ideas by exploring one aspect of the question.

> People continually debate the negative consequences of television violence on children. But who talks about the potential positive effects of criminal characters and actions on young audiences? Television villains are usually portrayed as vile, ugly characters who have no appeal to the audience. Television scripts usually have the bad character lose in the end of the program. This reinforces the idea that criminals are undesirable people and that their demise is a positive event. People worry that children will emulate violent characters on television, but I believe that television shows those characters pay for their actions, often with their lives. This is not the kind of message that encourages a child into a life of violence. Instead of always looking for the harm in television violence, we might also consider the good it does for the social education of young audiences.

In both paragraphs the writer refers to two ideas in the same paragraph. Each idea highlights or sets the background for the analysis of the other idea. This technique is very effective in bringing a unique perspective to the ideas discussed in the paragraphs.

Statement and Support

In a **statement and support** organization, the paragraph normally begins with a clear, strong statement. This statement is followed by examples, logic, or other details that support the statement.

The following paragraph is an example of a statement and support method of organization:

> It may be difficult to trace each incident of violence in society specifically to the effects of television violence. However, television violence creates a culture in which violence becomes acceptable behavior within a given society. Last year, the world was shocked by the violent behavior of American soldiers in the Abu Ghraib prison in Iraq. The most surprising fact about the case was that the soldiers involved were normal American men and women. However, many psychologists interviewed about those events stated unambiguously that those normal people behaved according to the culture they were exposed to as prison guards, a culture of disrespect, ridicule, and contempt for prisoners. Eventually, this abhorrent behavior seemed like normal behavior. If television continuously bombards society with violence, it will also begin to seem like normal, acceptable behavior.

Practice 4: Organizing Paragraphs

Read the following sample SAT prompt. Then write three paragraphs in response to the prompt. Organize one paragraph as a **cause and effect** paragraph, another either **comparing or contrasting** ideas, and the third as a **statement and support** paragraph.

> Think carefully about the issue in the quotation and the assignment below.
>
> *Character is like a tree and reputation like its shadow. The shadow is what we think of it; the tree is the real thing. – Abraham Lincoln*
>
> **Assignment**: Do you think that teenagers are too concerned about reputation and not concerned enough about character? Plan and write an essay in which you develop your point of view (opinion) on the issue. Support your opinion with reasons and evidence brought from your own experience, your studies, or your observations.

Using Convincing Language

The language used in persuasive essays is fundamental to the overall impact of the essay. If you were to try to persuade your friends and fellow students to boycott a product such as Lovely Lady Mascara because the product was tested on animals, you would probably consider your language very carefully. You would not simply say, "Lovely Lady, Inc. uses animals to test their products." This statement may not have much of an impact. However, if you were to use words to evince images of what of animal testing is like, you would probably have more success in convincing your friends of your point of view. This section will look at three ways to put more impact in the language you use in your SAT persuasive essay: **appeal to emotion**, **appeal to authority**, and **appeal to logic**.

Appeal to Emotion

The example of the animal testing issue above shows that the use of **emotional language** can have a greater impact on a reader than simple statements, because you involve the reader's emotions. While a picture is worth a thousand words, feelings can sometimes be worth a million. Consider the following two paragraphs about the issue of mandatory life jackets in recreational boating.

Factual Language	Emotional Language
Most attempts to make life jacket use mandatory for recreational boaters have failed. Not only boaters, but also boat manufacturers, and even life jacket manufacturers have opposed the idea. Boaters feel a law such as this would impinge on their personal freedom. They cite discomfort and inconvenience in having to wear these jackets at all times while boating. So far, no one has been able to propose a bill that is acceptable to all parties involved. Meanwhile, over 700 boating deaths occur every year, many due to a lack of personal floating devices. 	Sometimes a good idea occurs to us after it's too late to put it to use. That may be the case for the loved ones of over 400 people who drown every year due to failure to use a personal flotation device. The same people who resist laws that mandate the use of PFDs, or life jackets, find themselves in shock and grief when their brothers or daughters or friends become victims of sudden changes in weather on the water. The time is now to think about passing laws that make life jacket use mandatory. The time is now to prevent any possibility of that summer vacation you've looked forward to all year ending with the devastating loss of a loved one.

The first paragraph above is a good, logical paragraph. It is factual, containing a statistic on boating deaths, and makes a clear point. The second paragraph, with its appeal to emotion, involves the reader more personally. Words such as "too late," "shock and grief," "brothers or daughters or friends," "summer vacation," and "devastating loss" evince images and feelings in the reader. In this way the reader becomes personally involved with the ideas discussed in the paragraph.

A word of caution about the use of emotional language: While an appeal to emotion is effective, it should be backed with fact and logic. Simply appealing to emotion can be manipulative and detracts from the validity of your writing. However, infusing a valid and factual argument with emotional language will not only have a greater impact in persuading your reader, it will make your writing more vivid and compelling.

Appeal to Authority

The expert opinion of a respected **authority** is highly effective in persuasive writing. When readers see that your opinion or point of view is shared by people who have expertise or experience in the field, they accept your ideas more readily. For instance, think about shopping for suntan lotion. One bottle promises you adequate sun protection, smells pleasant, and is reasonably priced. Another bottle also promises adequate sun protection, smells pleasant, and is reasonably priced. The second bottle, however, features the words, "This product is approved by the National Association of Dermatologists." Chances are, you will chose the second bottle, because, all other things being equal, it carries the backing of an expert authority.

In persuasive writing, an authority should be **an acknowledged expert** in the field of your topic. It can also be individuals who have a unique experience of the topic — one that most people do not have access to. This kind of authority is called a **testimonial**. For instance, an individual who has experienced the beginning of skin cancer possibly because of frequent, unprotected exposure to the sun would have a kind of authority on the experience of cancer. Other forms of authority in persuasive writing can be organizations (such as the NAD).

An authority *cannot* be simply a person that people know because he or she is famous. The person must either be a specialist in the field or someone who has unique, firsthand experience. Nor is it effective to use people who simply have an interest. For instance, given the choice of the two tanning lotions mentioned above, if one were endorsed by "California Teens for Tans," while the other was recommended by the National Association of Dermatologists, you would probably put more trust in the latter.

The following two paragraphs are examples of valid appeals to authority. One uses the testimonial of a person with a unique experience, and the other uses the authority of an acknowledged expert in the field.

Testimonial	Acknowledged Expert
Today, the incidence of melanoma, a form of skin cancer, is steadily increasing. Dermatologists conclude this is due to a proliferation of tanning beds and their use among teenagers. Recently, my friend Josie wrote a cautionary editorial in the school newspaper. She had gone to tanning beds regularly since she was a freshman and although she had suffered sun poisoning a few times, did not stop. She wanted to look good. It wasn't until she became a senior and had a malignant mole removed from her arm that she stopped her habit. "I'm fine now," she told me, "but my dermatologist told me to stay out of the sun — and away from tanning beds."	Today, the incidence of melanoma, a form of skin cancer, is on the increase. And the ages of the people suffering from this life-threatening disease is decreasing. Dermatologists blame the burgeoning popularity of tanning beds for this trend. I saw a recent PBS documentary in which a dermatologist talked about the risks of tanning beds. When asked the question, she reacted strongly. "You don't even want to ask me about those beds." Ten years ago, she said, she dealt with melanoma cases in people in their 40s and 50s. Now, she is referring young people in their teens and 20s to oncologists (doctors who specialize in cancer). And, she said, "I know it is largely because of tanning beds."

The appeal to authority in the first paragraph is the testimonial of an individual who has had a unique experience of the topic of your paragraph. Not everyone can comment on the distressing experience of being faced with skin cancer. Those who can are the ones who have lived through it. Their experience does not make them cancer experts, but it does make them experts in the experience of facing the disease.

The second paragraph appeals to the authority of a recognized expert in the field of skin diseases, a dermatologist. She is a professional in the field and has years of experience in working with people with skin problems. Her authority on the subject supports your point of view.

Appeal to Logic

Emotion and authority strengthen your arguments. Reason and **logic** provide basic validity. A reader may not be able to relate to some feelings; she may also disagree even with an expert. But sound, logical reasoning is difficult to refute.

Arguments must consist of legitimate reasoning. Legitimate reasoning leads to sound conclusions, not just speculation. The two main processes of logical reasoning are **inductive reasoning** and **deductive reasoning**. **Chapter 3, Critical Thinking**, delves into these forms of logic in more detail. For the purposes of this chapter, we will look at the basic properties of each and discuss how they form valid arguments.

Inductive Reasoning

Inductive reasoning follows a line of thought leading **from specific details to a general idea**. It moves from the **concrete** (examples and facts) to the **abstract** (general idea). Look at the following example:

- **Fact**: The most serious injuries from skateboarding occur when a skateboarder falls and hits his or her head on pavement. This trauma can cause concussion and death.
- **Fact**: Ninety percent of serious skateboarding injuries occur to the unprotected head and to unprotected body joints.

Conclusion: The use of knee and elbow pads and helmets will decrease the incidence of serious injury due to skateboarding accidents.

- **Fact**: Studies have shown that students who invest 10 – 15 hours into test preparation time may increase their SAT scores by an average of 20 percent.
- **Example**: Sheila B. Smarter increased her SAT essay score by 23% after studying a book on the SAT essay.

Conclusion: Investing time in test preparation will lead to higher SAT scores.

Inductive reasoning, as illustrated by these examples, uses **specific** examples and details to arrive at **general** conclusions or principles.

DEDUCTIVE REASONING

Deductive reasoning follows a line of thought from **a general statement to a specific conclusion**. It takes a principle or idea and applies it to specific incidents. Look at the following examples.

> - **General Statement**: All skateboarders fall off their boards at least once as a beginner.
> - **Fact:** Dwane Fine is an advanced skateboarder.
>
> **CONCLUSION**: Duane Fine has fallen off his board at least once.

> - **General Statement**: All college-bound high school seniors must take the SAT or equivalent.
> - **Fact:** I am a college-bound high school senior.
>
> **CONCLUSION**: I will have to take the SAT or equivalent.

As you can see from the examples above, deductive reasoning *uses specific examples and facts to support general principles or ideas.*

TIP

Use appeals to emotion and appeals to authority in your persuasive writing; but use them within a strong context of logic and reason.

Practice 5: Inductive and Deductive Reasoning

Read the following examples of inductive and deductive reasoning. Then write on the lines provided whether each example is *inductive* or *deductive* reasoning and whether the conclusion reached is reasonable or unreasonable.

1. Student council members support providing more parking spaces for seniors. My friend Jim is a student council member. Therefore, my friend Jim supports providing more parking spaces for seniors.

   Inductive or deductive reasoning: ____________________

2. More owls are killed each year by eating mice poisoned with pesticides. The use of pesticides is increasing by 15% every year. Therefore, the owl population is facing a greater risk of death by poisoning every year.

   Inductive or deductive reasoning: ____________________

3. Thirty percent of fatal car accidents are caused by drunk driving. Driver's Education programs have decreased the incidence of car accidents caused by drunk driving. Therefore, Driver's Education saves lives.

   Inductive or deductive reasoning: ____________________

4. Running and jumping promotes alertness, brings more oxygen to the body, and increases clarity of thinking. Clarity, oxygen, and alertness are necessary for success in taking exams. Therefore, a month on track and field for every student before exams should be mandatory.

   Inductive or deductive reasoning ______________________________

PERSONAL EXPERIENCE AS SUPPORTIVE DETAIL

You are not expected to always be able to produce facts, figures, and current or historical events as support for your main ideas. Your **personal experience** and **observations** about life can also be valid support for your arguments. For instance, suppose you are given an essay prompt in which you are asked to discuss the value of making mistakes. You might remember a time when you were struggling with Algebra II. Write about how all the little mistakes you made caused you to be so frustrated that you determined all the more to be very careful. Write about how you sought more and more help from your parents, your teacher and your tutor. And write about how you salvaged your mark to a solid B by the end of the class, through pure determination to learn from your mistakes — and how your new study habits still benefit you.

Here are some more examples:

- You are writing about how sometimes knowledge comes from painful experience: You refer to your friend Josie's experience with tanning beds and what she learned from painful experience (see page 24).
- You are writing about the value of property ownership: You cite your experience of owning your own car. You write about how nothing has ever taught you more about taking care of an object. You mention how nothing has ever influenced you more to learn responsibility; and you mention how nothing has taught you more about economics.
- You are writing about the importance of choosing a profession based on what you love rather than on economics: you write about your uncle, who chose a profession in business administration while his passion was for teaching. You cite how he was a wealthy but disappointed man until he left his well paid job to earn a master's degree in teaching. Now, he takes fewer vacations to the Riviera, but he is always happy when you see him.

You are yourself an authority on life, by virtue of your own experience and observation. The college board SAT essay administrators acknowledge this. Use your experience, but be sure to present it by adhering to the principles outlined in this chapter.

> Remember: The SAT essay requires you to support your ideas with evidence based on <u>your own experience and observations</u>, as well as on other details and facts.

Practice 6: Personal Experience as Supportive Detail

As a practice in relating ideas to personal experience, read through the sample writing prompts in Appendix **A (p.).** Give yourself only a minute to brainstorm and jot down a possible personal experience that would be relevant to the concepts in each prompt. You don't have to develop the personal experience idea; this activity is designed to practice relating your own life experience to general ideas under discussion.

Chapter 1 Review: Writing Paragraphs

A. Reviewing Concepts. Answer the following questions on a separate piece of paper.

1. Name the three types of sentences found in a well written paragraph and the function of each.
2. Which two questions about the topic of a paragraph does a good topic sentence answer?
3. A good topic sentence should perform which two functions?
4. What is the function of good supporting sentences?
5. What are three ways in which you can support your topic sentence with details?
6. What are the three characteristics of good supporting sentences?
7. Name the two functions of a concluding sentence in a paragraph.
8. Name three ways in which an effective paragraph can be organized.
9. What is meant by emotional appeal? Why is it effective in persuasive writing?
10. What is an appeal to authority? What are two kinds of authority used in persuasive writing?
11. What are two forms of logical reasoning?
12. How do the two forms of logical reasoning differ from each other?

B. Paragraph practice. Write one paragraph of at least 5 sentences in response to the following sample SAT prompt. Then complete the activities below.

> Think carefully about the issue in the quotation and the assignment below.
>
> *Adolescence is society's permission slip for combining physical maturity with psychological irresponsibility.* – *Terri Apter, psychologist*
>
> **Assignment.** Do you believe that much of the conflict in adolescence is due to a combination of physical maturity and psychological immaturity? Plan and write an essay in which you develop your point of view (opinion) on the issue. Support your opinion with reasons and evidence brought from your own experience, your studies, or your observations.

Refer to the model paragraph on pages 12 – 13 for an example of the following activities:

1. Underline the topic sentence and concluding sentence.
2. Number each of the sentences in the paragraph.
3. On a separate paper, write how each sentence contributes to the paragraph.
4. Exchange your paragraph with a partner. Discuss what you have each written. If possible, add to each other's ideas, reinforce them, or suggest alternatives.

C. Diagnosing Paragraphs. Read the following three paragraphs. List the flaws in logic, organization, and effectiveness in each. Rewrite the paragraphs so that they are well organized and effective. (Be assertive. Revisions may need to be extensive.)

Paragraph 1

I believe that young adults are responsible enough to drink alcohol at age 18. After all, 18-year-olds can drive, and therefore they are considered responsible by society. Also, teens can vote when they are 18 years old. They have the right to decide who will run their governments and who will make their laws. This means that they are responsible people. If they are mature people, they are responsible people. If they are able to chose who will run their country, it seems that they should be able to choose what kinds of substances they can put in their own bodies. After all, they have to live with their bodies, and it is their right to take care of them or not. Furthermore, alcohol can be healthy if taken in small amounts.

Paragraph 2

I believe that young adults are responsible enough to be able to drink alcohol at age 18. I have an older sister, and when she was 18, she drank alcohol whenever she wanted to. When she drove home from a party, she knew which roads to take to avoid the police. She also was responsible enough to drive slowly when she had had some alcohol. My sister is a very responsible person. She is going to a good college and maintaining a B average. She hopes to be a cardiologist one day. People think that if 18-year-olds are allowed to drink alcohol, they will drink irresponsibly, speed in their cars, and cause fatal accidents. These fears, I feel, are based on the typical parental tendency to worry. They are not relevant, because there are a lot of teenagers like my sister. And she has never been arrested for underage drinking.

Paragraph 3

I believe that young adults are responsible enough to be able to drink alcohol at age 18. I recently read a book by a health professional who stated that a glass of wine each day can help prevent heart disease. My father suffers from heart disease, and it is a frightening condition. You never know if your heart may fail you any moment. When teenagers turn 18, they usually have a high school education. They have had many classes in health and physical fitness. They have had many years of training, through the school system's health and prevention programs, in the dangers of drugs and alcohol. They have been steeped in warnings about cigarette smoking and even secondary cigarette smoke. In general, 18-year-olds are well educated and well informed about personal health and safety. They are old enough and well equipped enough to act responsibly, based on that training and education. And responsible action is the most important qualification for the right to drink.

Chapter 2
Appropriate Vocabulary and Point of View

What aggravates you when you read? For many people, reading old phrases and worn out words aggravates them to yawn or sneer at the tired, recycle-bin words. Read the following paragraph, and think about your reaction to the language in it.

> *Beyond a shadow of a doubt, voting is a poorly understood and underused thing. I know you feel as though your vote just does not count. Often it doesn't. Have we ever been completely bowled over by the results of an election day? Or do we feel as though we have jumped from the frying pan into the fire? Has anyone felt the outcome of a vote was crucial to their nine-to-five life? I know a little knowledge can be a dangerous thing, but knowing how voting affects you is very important. As former President Harry Truman explained, "The buck stops here."*

The writing contains overused phrases and vague words. It expresses an opinion but in a way that is uninspired and too informal to be convincing or appealing. Also, the point of view changes midway through the idea, causing the writing to be unclear.

In writing for the SAT essay, you will want to

- **Avoid Trite Phrases and Overused Words**
- **Use Vivid, Specific Language**
- **Build a Vibrant Writing Vocabulary**
- **Develop and Maintain a Consistent Point of View**

A section entitled "Student Resources: Web sites and Books" is at the end of this chapter. In it, you will find resources for each of the above topics. These materials are rated for usefulness and ease of use.

TRITE PHRASES AND OVERUSED WORDS

Another term for clichéd language is "trite." These old, too-common phrases — for example "clear as glass" or "so it goes" — may cause readers to grow bored or put the text down in frustration. Words that are considered by editors and teachers to be overused are called "vague" and are not specific or vivid enough to add to reader enjoyment of the text. "Thing," "every," "seems to" and "just like" are examples of this language, which many wish would fall into a landfill of exhausted language, never to return.

Trite phrases and overused words are common problems for writers, but can be easily fixed. See below for the paragraph about voting; this time the trite phrases and overused words will be bolded.

> ***Beyond a shadow of a doubt***, *voting is a poorly understood and under used* ***thing***. *I know you feel as though your vote* ***just*** *does not count for* ***anything***. *Often it doesn't. Have we ever been completely* ***bowled over*** *by the results of an election day? Or do you feel as though we have* ***jumped out of the frying pan and into the fire***? *Has anyone felt that the outcome of a vote was interesting to their* ***nine-to-five*** *existence? I know that* ***a little knowledge can be a very dangerous thing***, *but knowing how or if voting affects you is* ***very important*** *— as the former President Harry Truman explained, "The buck stops here."*

Next, this paragraph will be shown rewritten with language which is original and specific.

> *Voting is a poorly understood and under used* ***tool for social change***. *I know you feel as though your vote does not count enough for* ***community action to take place and for changes to occur***. *Often it doesn't. Have the results of an election day ever completely* ***energized and invigorated*** *us? Has anyone felt that the outcome of a vote was* ***vital*** *to their* ***daily existence***? *I know that* ***being informed in a superficial way can be harmful***, *but knowing how voting affects you is* ***the right and duty of all citizens*** *— as the former President Harry Truman cried, "The buck stops here."*

The writing is clearer and has a forthright message. This type of writing could allow you to receive a passing score on the SAT. Still, it lacks a vivid approach. The following example brings in new phrases and comparisons to make the language vivid.

> *A regrettable fact is that voting has become the shallow option of popular opinion. Citizens may spout opinions like whales spout water, yet they do not make the effort to vote as their conscience dictates. Sadly, a majority of Americans feel as though their votes do not make a difference anymore. Too often, the lack of voting makes this feeling a bleak reality. When has the non-violent change of power on election day energized our country? When have we felt a vote's outcome to be a reflection of and foundation for our daily lives? Citizens understand the vast pool of information they must tap to vote effectively, but still shy away from such responsibility. We must reclaim the birthright of voting and turn to the business of protecting our rights through casting votes. As President Harry Truman said in regards to responsibility, "The buck stops here."*

This paragraph contains writing which would earn you an outstanding score on the SAT essay. Take a moment to consider the vivid language and specific word choices. For example in the second sentence, you will find a simile: "Citizens may spout opinions like whales spout water." Using some (but not too much) figurative language will add imagery to your essay. Specific word choice and vivid language will bolster all your writing.

There are lists of vague words and trite phrases to be found on the internet or in popular grammar handbooks (see the end of the chapter). The following section has a few examples of these vague words and trite phrases. These examples are intended to give you a broader idea of the kinds of words and phrases to avoid in your writing.

TRITE PHRASES

avoid it like the plague	put in a nutshell
better late than never	sad but true
cool as a cucumber	set the world on fire
cry over spilt milk	sneaking suspicion
dead as a doornail	spread like wildfire
fresh as a daisy	to coin a phrase
leave well enough alone	trial and error
moving experience	worth its weight in gold
point with pride	it's not rocket science

Practice 1: Trite Phrases

Look the list of trite phrases. Choose six and on a separate sheet of paper explain each phrase's meaning. You may use illustrations along with your text.

Practice 2: Creating Original Phrases

It is your turn "to coin a phrase." Choose eight phrases from the list above (or ones that you did not use in Practice 1), and rewrite them to mean the same concept but in your own words, using your own imagery and imagination.

Use eight index cards for this practice. On each card, write one phrase from the list on one side and then enter your rewrite on the other side. Partner with a classmate. For each card, show the side with your rewrite to your classmate and see if your classmate can name the phrase from the list you are recreating. Congratulate each other on every correct match and discuss how any mismatched pair could be made clearer. (Ex. quick as lightning = The vote was over quick as a camera flash.)

Overused Words and Select Synonyms

Selecting just the right word is easier with the use of a well-organized thesaurus, with a wide variety of word choices. The following list of overused words includes *possible* synonyms. Control over the word choice is yours as the writer to decide which synonym best suits the context in which you are writing.

When reading this list, pay careful attention to the bolded overused words, which are targeted as those which make readers cross their eyes with boredom. They are Overused, Overdone, and Obnoxious — do whatever you must do to avoid using these words. Replace these with appropriate synonyms.

Overused Words / Effective Synonyms	
Awesome:	stupendous, fabulous, outstanding
Beautiful:	alluring, attractive, exquisite, gorgeous, stunning, appealing
Begin:	launch, commence, originate, initiate, introduce
Big:	huge, immense, enormous, massive
Finish:	conclude, cease, achieve, deplete, complete
Good:	competent, virtuous, satisfactory, serviceable
Important:	notable, critical, significant, meaningful, vital
Interesting:	appealing, absorbing, entertaining, fascinating
Like (adj):	equivalent, similar, parallel
Like (verb):	appreciate, enjoy, relish
Nice:	charming, pleasant, satisfying
Try:	venture, endeavor, attempt
Very:	extremely, unusually, exceedingly

Launch

Practice 3: Saying No to Trite Phrases and Overused Words

Read the following excerpt of a political speech. Some trite phrases and overused words have been bolded. After reading the speech, rewrite the sections with bolded text with original phrasing and words.

My Fellow Citizens,

This is a **very great day** for our community — it is a validation of all we hold dear in our corner of **America's vast heartland**. We are here today **in one accord** to ratify a local ordinance: an ordinance which you asked for and which you used your freedom of choice to vote for. Your freedom of expression rings out as loud and clear as the Liberty Bell, **setting the world on fire** for Democracy.

Take my word for it, as a **humble public servant** who has only **great** respect for you — you, who are **true Americans**. You are the **promise of our nation**, and

I can **point with pride** to you who have voted and supported the **worthy cause** of Democracy. Your loyalty to its **awesome** standard will help it **spread like wildfire** around the globe. And it is the **thing** at work for you today.

Today I am honored by your presence and the presence of **those who have gone before me in the pursuit of life and liberty**. To live in this **very great** nation is **truly** to already have found happiness. So join with me as I put my signature to this **important new** ordinance, developed after much **trial and error,** which says "no persons may possess any pyrotechnic ignition mechanisms, excepting in July." We plan to **avoid** fireworks **like the plague**.

I **promise** everyone here will feel **just** that much safer in our **homeland** with the new ordinance which guarantees walking in the park or attending a speech rally with no fears of Roman candles, pop rockets, or even firecrackers, thwarting our citizens' desires for peace and prosperity. This is **a moving experience**. Thank you from the **bottom of my heart**.

Practice 4: Tossing Out Trite Phrases and Overused Words

Consider your writing. Are there words or phrases you tend to use without thinking? Write an opinion paragraph using one of the topics below. First, form a definite opinion about the topic, then focus on using specific words and new phrases to explain. Look over your words when you are finished. Are there any which should go in the recycle bin? If so, replace them.

Time for Voting for Class President (during or after school?)

Voting for Favorite Lunch (your choice)

Closing School on Election Day (good or bad idea?)

Amendment "Save Insects" (would you even vote?)

Amendment "Ban Student Parking" (for/against)

Vote for Best Teacher (your vote?)

Build a Writing Vocabulary

The word **"vocabulary"** is based on the Latin root word *voca-*, meaning **to call**. Voc- is the Latin root for several other words, including: *advocate*, *convoke*, *evocative*, *invoke*, *provocation*, *vocal*, *vocation*, *vociferous*, *and voice*. Knowing the Latin root word voc-, is a clue to the meaning of all these words and more.

The Latin word vocabulum, meaning "name," gives the word "vocabulary" its full form. Vocabulary's different definitions are:

(1) a body of words used in a specific language or discipline
(2) the body of words known to a particular person (written and spoken)
(3) a list of words with the meanings given.

Notice that in the second definition, "vocabulary" refers to both the written and spoken words known to an individual. Most people have a larger written vocabulary than a spoken one. Seeing words as we write them gives us connections to other words we know. Voicing words aloud does not offer the same connections. Use these connections in your own writing by studying Latin and Greek root words. You may also want to scan lists of words for memorizing by sight, but understanding how to use root words expands your vocabulary faster and gives you more flexibility in reasoning out the meanings of new words.

In the section offering resources at the end of this chapter, you will find materials focusing on vocabulary building. Using these materials will give you a good foundation for building your own writing vocabulary.

Practice 5: Building a Writing Vocabulary

A. The list below contains common root words in both Latin and Greek, with their meanings. On your own paper, write down all the words you know which are built from each root word. You should be able to write at least five. If you cannot create five new words, look up the root word in the dictionary and find as many as you can to write down. When you finish, compare lists with your class. Which words are most commonly known and which are unusual?

Root	Meaning	Example
amor-	love	amorous
annu, anni	year	anniversary
demo-	people	democracy
mar-	sea	marine
pan-	all	panorama
port-	door or gate	portable
soli, solo	one or alone	solitary

B. For one of the five words you created from each of the eight given root words, write a sentence using the new word correctly. You will have a total of eight sentences.

C. Using the vocabulary you've found in model written essays will also reinforce what you learn. Write two opinion paragraphs using any of the ten topics below. Consider your word choices carefully, using new vocabulary from resources found in the section at the end of this chapter and make connections to other words you already know. Share your paragraphs with your teacher or class.

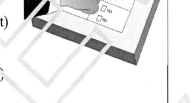

Electoral College (outdated or relevant)

Voting Assistance for First-Time Voters (should taxpayers pay for this?)

Electronic Voting Machines (benefit or bane)

Listing of Candidates on Ballots (alphabet or other way)

Age Limits on Voting (your choice)

Political Polling at Voting Sites (total ban or not)

Political Commercials (pro/con)

New Symbols for Political Parties (your choice)

Allow Foreign-Born President? (yes or no)

Who Would You "Write-in" for Your State Governor?

DEVELOP AND MAINTAIN A CONSISTENT TONE AND POINT OF VIEW

When you write, you need to decide what type of voice or **point of view** you wish to use. This is an important decision, because it affects the **tone** and the **logic** of your writing. Consciously choosing a point of view is also important because an essay must have the same point of view throughout to receive a good grade.

Point of view is the stance you want to take when communicating with your audience. Would you want to address them personally with the "I" pronoun, or with a direct approach using the pronoun "you," or with a balanced reporting style using the pronoun "they?"

The readers of the SAT essays will be looking for clear opinions. They will also expect a formal and objective (balanced or factual) tone. Most importantly, they will look for a consistent point of view, which communicates the objective, formal tone.

Tone refers to the way a writer uses words to present a certain attitude or feeling to the reader. For example, you would probably use a subjective or biased tone when composing a letter to the editor about an issue you care about:

> *"With spyware and viruses attacking e-mails by the most insidious methods yet devised, I am fleeing to the old tried-and-true method for letters: stamp 'em, seal 'em, and drop 'em in a box. At least you know the post office won't be phishing for your identity or embedding viruses to erase your hard drive. And stamps, with the imagination put into them, are inspiring even when paying bills. Plus the mystery of when the letter will arrive at its destination is a thriller. We can use this little thrill in our lives."*

But when writing a report about the same issue, you want to use an objective or factual tone:

"Today's e-mails are challenged by ingenious advertisers and eager entrepreneurs. The wise consumer knows to exercise caution when opening unknown communications. Or the consumer may choose to use the traditional source of sending correspondence, the postal service. While it is not as quick, it has advantages in security and in the possibility of collecting stamps."

You can see that the verbs and adjectives in the first example communicate a biased tone of danger and dread for electronic messaging while using a folksy tone to describe the post office method. The use of the pronoun "we" in the last sentence brings the reader into a supposed agreement with the writer. In the second example, the writer chooses mild words to describe the e-mail problem and notes both advantages and disadvantages to using the mail service. It reports facts. For an opinion essay you could use a biased, pleading tone, but since the SAT essay requires that you support your opinion, you would need to keep a reasonably factual (or objective) tone.

The most ineffective way to communicate an opinion objectively is to use the **first-person point of view**: that is, by using *I*, *me*, or *my* statements. Using the first person makes the essay sound informal and subjective or based on feelings instead of evidence. It is acceptable as long as it is consistent and stays on topic. The first-person point of view is most acceptable when using details based upon the writer's personal experiences which support the opinion. If you begin an essay with first-person point of view, you should continue with it throughout the essay.

Another way to objectively communicate an opinion is by using the second-person point of view; that is, by directly addressing the reader as "you." With second person, the writer or speaker gives his audience a command, a plea, or sometimes even a criticism. Be aware, though, that speaking directly to the reader, when not handled carefully, can come across as insulting to the reader's intelligence.

The most effective way to produce an essay which is both objective, formal, and pleasing is the **third-person point of view**: that is, by using *they*, *he*, *she*, *their*, or *them* statements. Using this point of view consistently creates a clear and logical communication with readers. They will most likely appreciate your ideas and will probably consider your opinion on the topic favorably.

Practice 6: Develop a Consistent Point of View

Read the following 3 paragraphs. As you read, decide which point of view (1st, 2nd, or 3rd person) is being used and if it is consistent. On your own paper, write whether it is first, second, or third person point of view. Then change the point of view by rewriting each paragraph and changing its pronouns. At the end of each paragraph, write which point of view it now has and how that affects the logic or tone of the paragraph. Be sure to use each point of view only once.

1. **Election Day Hold-Outs**

E-mails, billboards, and mass mailings: are these always created to herald a new product which will make life easier and more joyous? No. Often, this lavish attention heaped upon citizens hails from local political campaign managers. Unfortunately, this avalanche of unfounded opinions and poorly phrased platforms is about to break the backs of the targeted constituency. No wonder people have stayed away from the polls in record numbers. The last local campaign reported that only 31% of registered voters made the trek to nearby voting sites. Part of the blame rests on the voting schedule: Tuesdays between 7 am and 7 pm. The old joke about "vote early and vote often" is a mockery in this scenario. Just voting that one Tuesday is almost impossible. Between reading campaign ads and traveling the daily work-commute, people cannot get to the polls that one time. Can other arrangements be made for the traditional voting hours on voting day? Some have suggested voting by e-mail. Others shudder at the thought of votes evaporating into cyberspace. But until a better arrangement is found, do not begrudge holdout voters — they are holding out their hopes for a chance to vote.

2. **Turn that Corner: Vote**

You know, Election Day is just a righthand turn down the next corner. For some, it may be a lefthand turn down the corner. Whatever the direction of your turn, it should lead you to your local polling site. You have been preparing for this day for weeks, but you have a vague feeling of uneasiness telling you that you should have spent the last few months or several months studying the full voting agenda: The agenda which shows the amendments, resolutions, and initiatives being voted upon this election. You know the main candidates and what they stand for, but do you know about the details concerning your local government? For example, how will you vote when you are faced with a hike in taxes for local schools? How will you vote when you're faced with the resolution to ban all dogs in local parks? How will you vote when you are faced with the Zero-Spam initiative? Ok, that last one is a no-brainer, but you must have a clear and focused stand on these issues and more when you stand in that mini-cubicle and you touch that screen, or you push that button, or you pull that lever. Take heart — you have made your first choice count — mentally, you are in the booth! Make sure you get there physically as well. Vote.

3. **A Clear Choice**

Some people believe our government should change to a one-party system, instead of the usual two or, less commonly, three. I say, leave us a choice. Take the party symbols for example. The traditional symbols of the two major political parties indicate that they have little in common, except that they are both animals. I mean, the symbols are animals: the donkey and the elephant. I can see the differences between them clearly. First, the donkey is a domesticated farm animal which is stubborn and works hard and then refuses to work hard. The donkey is short with comically large ears — but I do not know if that means he hears better than other animals or not. When the humblest sort of work must be done, say scraping a field flat or hauling a load of wood for a fire — the donkey is my choice. Now the elephant is a domesticated animal as well, though not as completely, some say. I watch elephants at the zoo, and I think of how wonderfully exotic they seem. At times, they wear chains on their legs as their immense size must be respected and a little feared. The elephant has the reputation of never forgetting, but what does it need to remember? With its size, who would argue a point of memory with an elephant? I have learned that elephants are willing to transport humans, whether they are maharajas or circus clowns. When a smattering of showmanship and sheer awesome power is called for — my choice is the elephant. One animal is suited to humble labor, the other to extreme displays — I say we need them both. And I vote for the two-party system to stay.

Practice 7: Maintain a Consistent Point of View

Think about your voice in communicating with readers. Your point of view will make a strong impact on your success when writing. Look back at Practice 5C. Choose a different topic from the list or create one of your own with your teacher's approval. Write an opinion paragraph using the point of view you feel most comfortable with and you think will help you in writing the SAT essay.

Focus on maintaining that point of view throughout your paragraph. When you are finished, you may exchange this paragraph with other students for peer review or you may ask your teacher for feedback.

Student Resources: Web sites and Books

Overused words

http://www.phschool.com/iText/wag/bronze/backmatter/OW_index.html

Part of the Pearson Prentiss Hall publisher's site, the section titled "Commonly Overused Words" is easy to use. The URL, though a bear to enter, is worth the trouble. There are links to Commonly Misspelled Words, an Abbreviation Guide, an Internet Resource Handbook, and more.

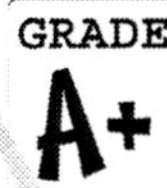

Clichés

http://www.westegg.com/cliche

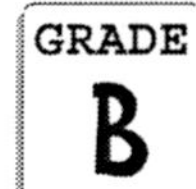

This search engine specializes in phrases that have been around since the dinosaurs. Accessing words that include chichés, phrases that might soon become old hat, and chiché origins can be done in no time flat. Over 3,000 worn-out or trite phrases — a king's ransom's worth — are included. Free as a bird to anyone on the Web.

Book:

Andrea Lunsford. The St Martin's Handbook: With 2003 MLA Update. 5th ed. New York: Bedford St. Martin's, 2003.

A popular textbook in freshman English courses and high schools alike, this most recent edition contains chapters on reading and note-taking, grammar, research, and citation, as well as improving your writing style by avoiding chichés and other common mistakes.

Building Vocabulary

http://www.wordfocus.com/

This site proudly proclaims, "Hello, come in and focus on English words derived from Latin and Greek sources!" Not the most contemporary or hip site on the Web, but a solid source of information regarding the heritage of everyday words descending from Latin and Greek languages. Several cross reference indexes also make the site worth the trip.

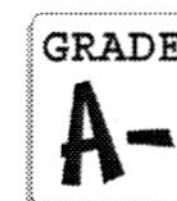

http://grammar.ccc.commnet.edu/grammar

A part of the excellent Guide to Grammar and Writing Web site, this site presents root words and word lists, but its strength lies in its links to a myriad of other sites which have vocabulary and word-of-the-day programs.

http://www.freevocabulary.com/

"5000 Collegiate Words with Brief Definitions." A truly mammoth source for SAT vocabulary words, it has limited definitions (ex: rabid is defined only as "being infected with rabies," while most sources define it first as "furious."), and there's no pronunciation guide or word history. It does fulfill its mission of presenting 5000 words online though, clearly presented in alphabetical order.

Chapter 2 Review

Part A.

Read the passage below, first for content, then for the use of point of view (1st, 2nd, 3rd person). Rewrite to create an effective, balanced, and consistent point of view. Think about which point of view would best communicate an effective essay, incorporating details and demonstrating a clear opinion. Also, eliminate and replace, when possible, any trite phrases or overused words with specific words and vivid language.

Rite of Passage

A rite of passage refers to an important event in your life that changes you in ways you will never understand nor appreciate. Take voting for instance. You refuse to believe that just the chore of voting will alter the course of your life? You could not be more mistaken! Try to imagine the awesome power people feel when pushing the button next to their candidate's name, knowing they control their own political voice in that very moment. The next day, they awaken to a beautiful broadcast news report that confirms their candidate has won the hard-fought election — O glory! Their opinions have won out over the clods in the opposing camp. This is a moving experience for you, too, since you voted for the big winner.

Now you march downstairs — proud as a peacock — you begin to measure coffee the way you like — I prefer it thick as tar, you fix the toaster, by trial and error, to the best setting — very dark and crunchy; you grab a grape jelly packet; and you sit at the kitchen table, as if you were a very important person, to listen to the radio as you wait to chow down. Contented and feeling good knowing that you are a winner, you then realize that you forgot to put in a coffee filter, your toaster is unplugged, your packet of jelly is old, and all that can be heard on the radio is the sobering, bad news of a ballot recount. Not one to cry over spilt milk, I would try to ignore that my candidate could lose.

But you face the day with energy and a lot of purpose — though you sense a clear and present danger in what you thought was your community. I mean, it takes a village to make life better, right? At school, although hungry and sleepy, the feeling of being part of a good political vote makes reality easier to take. I know you can fool a lot of the people a lot of the time. And this was one of those times. Nobody likes being a loser — they avoid the idea like the plague. The next day, your candidate concedes the election, admitting to voting goofs. You know, they say that what doesn't kill you makes you stronger. I call this a rite of passage.

Part B

This chapter has reviewed material about appropriate and creative vocabulary use and a consistent point of view. Look back once more to Practice 5C. Choose a topic about which you have not yet written, or create a new topic with your teacher's approval.

Write an opinion essay of three to four paragraphs on your chosen topic, focusing on using both appropriate vocabulary and a consistent point of view. Remember to avoid overused words and trite phrases. You may use a dictionary and thesaurus for this review.

Chapter 3
Critical Thinking

Some of the most important work you will do when faced with your SAT essay prompt will be done even before your pencil touches paper. Before you begin formulating your thesis, supporting ideas, and conclusion, you will apply the two most vital skills a persuasive writer can have: **careful reading** and **critical thinking**.

The ability to read carefully and the ability to think critically are essential in producing a quality essay. In this session, we will discuss them individually as components of an overall approach to essay writing. In this chapter, we will step back from essay writing mechanics and explore the thinking and reading skills crucial for producing clear and reasonable ideas. The goal is to encourage you in developing and shaping sentences, paragraphs, and other mechanical aspects of essay writing.

Because the techniques of careful reading and critical thinking center around examining ideas rather than merely accepting them, you can practice these techniques in many areas of your life. By doing so, you will make them an automatic part of your thinking process by the time you take your SAT essay exam.

First, we will look at basic skills involved in careful reading, especially in regards to the SAT essay prompt. Then we will discuss some of the skills and intellectual characteristics involved in critical thinking.

Careful Reading

Critical thinking begins with careful reading. You have already read several standard-form SAT prompts and assignments in the first two chapters of this book. You probably feel you know their standard format by heart and are ready to skip them. But have you read them carefully? One clue that can indicate whether or not you have is a visual one. Look at the directions and prompts you have read in this book so far. Are there any pencil marks on them? If so, and if they underline key words or show question marks and/or other notes in the margins, then you've probably read those words carefully.

If not, however, don't worry. You may be hesitant to mark up a book, but do not hesitate to mark the prompt on your test. Marking a passage is an effective tool in careful reading, which you will learn in the next section.

Now we look at the three sections of the SAT essay directions, the **general directions**, the **prompt**, and the **assignment**, and how we can read them as carefully as possible.

Careful Reading of The General Directions

A **critical thinker** is an independent analyst of ideas, but in following directions that will lead you to an excellent essay score, you must turn from critical thinking and become a strict interpreter of words and a close adherent to their meanings. Reading the directions of the SAT essay is not a time for creative, critical, or even magical thinking! Following them greatly increases your chances of a good score.

In the text box below are general directions for writing an SAT essay. Read them carefully, underlining any key ideas, words, or phrases you wish.

> The essay gives you an opportunity to show how effectively you can develop and express ideas. You should therefore take care to develop your point of view, present your ideas logically and clearly, and use language precisely.
>
> Your essay must be written on the lines provided on your answer sheet — you will receive no other paper on which to write. You will have enough space if you write on every line, avoid wide margins, and keep your handwriting to a reasonable size. Remember that people who are not familiar with your handwriting will read what you write. Try to write or print so that what you are writing is legible to those readers.
>
> You have twenty-five minutes to write an essay on the topic assigned below. DO NOT WRITE ON ANOTHER TOPIC. AN OFF-TOPIC ESSAY WILL RECEIVE A SCORE OF ZERO.

Now that you have read and underlined key ideas in the directions, briefly answer the following seven questions.

1. What is the purpose of writing the essay?
2. What three things should you do in the essay to accomplish this purpose?
3. Where will you write the essay?
4. Can you ask for extra paper if you run out?
5. What advice was given to help ensure enough room to write the essay?
6. How can you make sure the reader is able to read your essay?
7. What happens if you don't stay on topic?

THE PROMPT DIRECTIONS

Now read the directions specific to the essay prompt. They are written as follows:

Think carefully about the issue presented in the following excerpt and assignment below:

1. What two words give the command in prompt directions? **Answer**: *Think carefully*. Before doing any other preparation for this essay, you are told what to do and how to do it. Think carefully. Don't start writing at the first thought that comes to mind. Once you read the whole prompt, try to imagine the essay as a whole. Jot down ideas and begin writing only after you have a good idea of what to say.

2. What will you be thinking about? **Answer**: *The issue*. The quote or excerpt, as well as the question given in the assignment, addresses a specific issue. You cannot simply respond to the quote without addressing the issue under discussion. You must clearly identify what that issue is.

3. Where is the issue presented? **Answer**: *In the excerpt AND in the assignment*. The excerpt provides a background idea. The assignment provides the specific question which defines the issue to be addressed. Keep the quote in mind as you read the assigned question.

CAREFUL READING OF THE PROMPT

The **prompt** consists of a quote or excerpt which discusses a topic. It can also consist of a short paragraph which describes an issue. The **excerpt, quote, or descriptive paragraph** sets you up for the **assignment**. You read it carefully, more than once, underlining key words and phrases. If it's a quote or an excerpt, consider who that said the words. Consider why they were said. What could the motive have been? Do you agree or disagree?

Remember, the prompt is to get you *started thinking*. It is not the exact question you will answer. That comes next.

The prompt we are working with consists of two quotes:

> *For it has been said so truthfully that it is the soldier, not the reporter, who has given us the freedom of the press. It is the soldier, not the poet, who has given us freedom of speech. It is the soldier, not the agitator, who has given us the freedom to protest.*
>
> – *Zell Miller, U.S. senator (GA) 2004*
>
> *See how the world its veterans rewards!*
> *A youth of frolics, an old age of cards.*
>
> –*Alexander Pope, poet (1688 – 1744)*

Discussion

1. The first quote in the prompt is about soldiers and their contributions to society. The second quote comments on the way "the world" rewards soldiers for their work. The two quotes together seem to point to a discrepancy between the heroic deeds of the soldier in safeguarding our freedoms and the repayment, or lack of it, that society provided a soldier.

2. The two quotes also portray two contrasting moods. The first quote portrays a triumphant one. It proclaims the commendable successes and achievements of the soldier defending his country. The second quote has a satirical tone. It identifies a regrettable situation. It describes veterans who have sacrificed for their countries being largely forgotten.

3. A third way of thinking about these two quotes is to look at the main details. The first quote mentions laudable qualities: freedom of speech, freedom of the press, freedom to protest, and liberty itself. These are elements of a vigorous, inspired, free, and growing society. The second quote, on the other hand, evinces an image of old age and playing cards. These are qualities of an ending of life and, of an activity that merely passes time, rather than using it to build a better world.

Your task, in thinking about these two quotes, is to begin to see the relationships between them, to ask yourself about their conflictive elements, and to consider how they might be reconciled.

Careful Reading of the Assignment

Here is the assignment part of the prompt:

> **Assignment**: How might society pay its debt of gratitude towards its soldiers? Plan and write an essay in which you develop your point of view on this issue. Support your position with reasoning and examples taken from your reading, studies, experience, or observations.

The assignment has two parts. The first part is the question you are to answer. The second part is a description of how you are to answer it. That description includes three instructions: **plan the essay, write the essay,** and **develop ideas** using evidence and supporting ideas from your own life. These instructions are discussed and illustrated in more detail in chapters 1 and 2. Here, we will do a careful reading of the question.

Here is the question with key words underlined: "**How might society pay its debt of gratitude towards its soldiers?**" The word **how** indicates that the essay will provide practical or creative ways to do something. The word **society** indicates who would do the action. Remember that society includes individuals as well as institutions, governments, and legal systems. The question refers to society's **debt** and assumes one exists. This assumption is not simply the bias of the test writer but is consistent with ideas presented with the quotes. Therefore, your essay must accept the same assumptions that the question does.

The word **gratitude** signals that the debt society owes is one of thankfulness for a gift or contribution. This may inspire you to think of what kinds of contributions soldiers make and how society might repay them. Remember, the focus of the question is not on *the contributions* but on how *they can be repaid.* Still, brainstorming the sacrifices of soldiers will give you ideas on answering that question.

Finally, the word **soldiers** indicates that it is not just soldiers who have fought in wars (veterans) but also those who stand ready or who are now fighting. You might think of all the ways in which society can support or repay soldiers at every step of their duty.

The above discussion is a careful reading of an 11-word sentence. It illustrates the way in which you can carefully read the question you are given on the SAT essay assignment.

Practice 1: Careful Reading

Read the following assignment question carefully. Underline all key words. Write a discussion of each key word using the model given in the previous section, "The Assignment."

> **Assignment:** To what extent is it necessary to sacrifice individual freedoms for the sake of the collective good?

Critical Thinking

Careful reading, like careful listening and careful observing, is the basis of critical thinking. In the examples of careful reading given in the previous section, you probably noticed that simply reading a short sentence carefully involved an active process of thinking. That is the beginning of **critical thinking**. In this section we will identify and discuss the more specific characteristics and skills involved.

Critical thinking means not automatically accepting everything you hear, read, or see. It means analyzing and thinking for yourself, looking beyond what is in front of you and wondering about possibilities not quite apparent. It does not mean finding fault, but is really about finding, to the extent possible, the truth behind appearances.

You have practiced critical thinking throughout your life, when it suited your purposes. The critical thinker is the two-year-old who has a "Why?" for everything she is told. When that two-year-old becomes a teenager, she may have a "Why not?" for everything she is told she cannot do. These somewhat droll examples underscore the fact that humans are natural critical thinkers. The purpose of this section is to explore critical thinking as a skill to be consciously developed by anyone who wants to grow intellectually and understand the world around him.

Characteristics of Critical Thinking

For your more immediate purposes, however, the ability to think critically will be an asset in writing the SAT essay. This is because the SAT essay is a piece of **persuasive writing**, for which critical thinking is essential. As we discuss the characteristics needed for critical thinking, you may discover you already practice critical thinking and how to extend the practice further, adding new skills to practice on a daily basis. Soon, critical thinking will become your natural way of thinking — your "default" thinking mode.

The aspects of critical thinking discussed in this chapter are shown here in a "mind map."

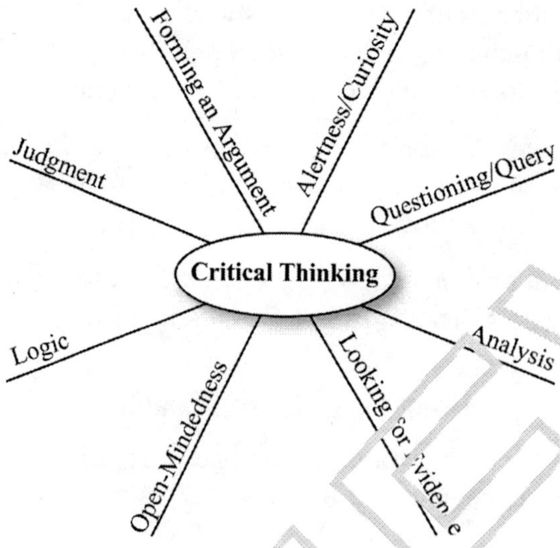

ALERTNESS/CURIOSITY

The first and basic requirement for critical thinking is **alertness** and the desire to **understand**. Alertness means being aware of the significance of what you are reading or being told. For example, If you heard your state legislature was debating a law prohibiting drivers under age 20 from driving with more than two people in the car, you would immediately become **alert** to that bill's impact on your life. You would be **curious** about the bill and want to learn more details. You might be prompted to contact your state representative for information and to register your concerns.

This alertness and curiosity is concerned with your personal life and situation. It is the beginning of critical thinking. A further step in critical thinking is expanding that alertness and curiosity into the more abstract realm of the society around you. This would prompt you to be alert that the new law might affect others, such as car pools that college students have formed to get to class or work. It might also affect the volume of cars on the road, traffic congestion, and air pollution. This would lead you to be curious about who is behind this bill and their motives. Now you are expanding your critical thinking skills from your own personal realm into a social and political arena which can eventually make a difference in society.

QUESTIONING/QUERY

Remember the child with the "Why?" for everything? Besides a budding critical thinker, she is also a potential journalist because the basic queries of journalism inform the queries of a critical thinker: Who, What, Where, When, Why, and How (the 5 Ws and H).

You need not systematically go through each query in turn, but once you become alert and curious about an issue and begin asking questions, at least some of these questions will immediately arise. For instance, with the issue of limiting the number of young people in a car, you began to wonder *how* it would affect you and others, *who* was behind the proposed law (some interest groups?) and *why* they were proposing it (when there are already too many cars on the road). The rest of the *W*s will undoubtedly make an appearance as you delve into the truth of any issue.

The "**Who**" query is the one that a critical thinker should primarily consider. As a student, you may not be in the habit of always thinking "Who wrote this?", because your text and assigned books are most likely produced by reputable authorship and educational publishing firms. But when doing research on the Internet, or reading periodicals and newspapers, it's important to be aware of the bias of writers and publishers. At the same time, determining who wrote the text you are reading can also lend credibility to its text. For instance, an article on the value to society of space exploration, written by a veteran astronaut, would have the credibility of an acknowledged professional.

The "**When**" is also a crucial query, especially in the 21st century, when information changes rapidly and new knowledge emerges daily. For example, you would not think of reading a computer manual that was written five years ago. And, while most literature is timeless in scope and relevant in all centuries, most technical, historical, and non-fiction writing is time sensitive, and should be considered as such.

Analysis

Asking questions ad speculating and researching answers begins the process of analyzing any text. Careful analysis involves all aspects of critical thinking, from careful reading to querying to defining terms to interpreting and applying information.

As a simple example, look at the second quote from the writing prompt on page 45:

See how the world its veterans rewards!
A youth of frolics, an old age of cards.

– Alexander Pope, poet (1688 – 1744)

By beginning with the basic journalistic questions we find out that the "**Who, When,** and **Where**" reveal an English poet of the 17th century. Pope's comments about veterans, then, we may question as to their relevance, by doing research into the welfare of American veterans today. For instance, we may find that a large enough percentage of Vietnam veterans are homeless, disabled, or financially disadvantaged to the extent of not being able to living fulfilling lives. This would lend validity to Pope's words, even across oceans and over centuries of time. As a poet, his words could be seen as a **metaphor**: an old age of playing of cards could represent a certain amount of emptiness, meaninglessness, and abandonment by society.

This is one valid interpretation of Pope's words, based on **query** and **research**. It requires a mind willing to take an active part in the "conversation" with the author, which may necessitate further research on the reader's part. All text, especially that which is written to persuade, should be read with this kind of active and probing frame of mind.

LOOKING FOR EVIDENCE

Another aspect of analyzing a text involves considering the evidence. How does the author support his or her statements? If the support is strong and clear, or if it can be proven through scientific study, then the main idea of the writing can usually be accepted. If you read an editorial in the newspaper which claims that American borders should be closed to immigrants except under rigorous and lengthy scrutiny because immigrants take jobs away from Americans, you would expect the writer to provide documented evidence to support his claims. The writer would have to include objective statistics that show Americans are losing jobs to immigrants who are not otherwise contributing to the American economy or culture.

Evidence is an essential part of arguments. Without it, for good or bad, arguments lose strength. Think about the power of television to present evidence of disasters and to mobilize people to act. Severe famines in Africa and Ethiopia had gone without significant outside help until, in the mid 1980s, television began bringing images of starving people to the West, mobilizing millions of ordinary citizens to send aid.

When reading any author's point of view, it is fair to require sufficient evidence in the form of **examples, statistics, historical events**, among others to support that viewpoint.

Practice 2: Looking for Evidence

Read the following paragraph. Underline the text which presents evidence of the main idea. Write an analysis of the evidence, stating if you think it is strong or weak, and why.

The duty of government is to protect the "inalienable rights" of citizens, not take them away. The great philosopher John Locke, whose ideas had more influence on the writing of the U.S. Constitution than anything else, stated that basic personal rights belong to individuals by birthright. They are not lent to them by the government as long as it serves the government's purposes. Locke, in his Treatises of Government, stated that the job of a citizen is to obey the laws of government, and the job of government is to protect the rights of citizens. The Constitution of our country is based on these standards. If the government takes away the personal freedoms of Americans, it would have, in effect, defied the principles upon which it and the country are founded.

OPEN-MINDEDNESS

One cannot be a critical thinker if one is a closed-minded thinker. Since the purpose of **critical thinking** is to develop understanding and expand knowledge through a discriminating thought process, there is no point in having your mind made up before you finish reading the text. On the other hand, critical thinking does not mean being gullible to every word in print. It means that a reader must reach a conclusion about the validity of a text only after subjecting it to the same kind of objective scrutiny any text should undergo.

As an example, imagine that a reader is adamant that all Muslims are terrorists. Imagine that reader reading an essay by a fellow student, who is Muslim, on the difficulties of living in the United States with a Muslim name because of racial profiling. That reader will tend to remain unchanged from reading this information. Instead, he or she will pass all steps of critical thinking and jump immediately to the final step of forming a conclusive argument: the same argument he or she has always had, that Muslims are not to be trusted.

Now, every reader, including our hypothetical, closed-minded one, is entitled to his opinion. However, if that opinion is foremost in a reader's mind, to the extent that he does not consider any new ideas or different angles on ideas, then that reader has remained unchanged through the whole process. This again is acceptable as a free citizen; it just does not constitute critical thinking. *Critical thinking is, by definition, an examination of ideas*. This examination may indeed lead a reader to confirm what he already believes. Or it may lead to new insights. Either way, the approach is most effective if it is open minded.

Logic

Chapter 1 of this book took a brief look at the basic forms of logic called inductive and deductive reasoning. Inductive and deductive reasoning are often implicitly used in persuasive writing, and a clear understanding of these reasoning processes will improve your ability to decipher an author's argument and evaluate its strengths and weaknesses. Chapter 1 showed how sound reasoning can lead to sound conclusions. Here we will discuss how flawed reasoning can lead to flawed — and sometimes dangerous — results.

We will first consider **inductive reasoning**, which uses specific statements to build a probable general conclusion or truth. One problem with accuracy in inductive reasoning occurs when the conclusion is based on at least one premise which is not "categorical," or exhaustive in its reach. Look at the following example:

> **First premise:** I have met several students from New York University.
> **Second premise:** All of them enjoyed going to parties.
> **Conclusion:** All NYU students are partiers.

The weakness in this conclusion comes from the fact that the statements, or premises, are not **categorical**. The first statement says that I have met "several" students from NYU. I have not met "all" of them. It is an equivocal statement, which can be read in two ways: (1) "I have met a small number of NYU students." and (2) "There are thousands of NYU students I have *never* met." Because this premise does not include *all* NYU students, an **unequivocal conclusion** about *all* of them and their recreational preferences cannot be reached. Words like "several," "most," and "many," when used in logical thinking should alert you to the possibility of unsound logic.

Unsound inductive reasoning can also come from making connections between facts that are not supported. This can be dangerous when used to make implications against people. The American justice system guards against this by devaluing **circumstantial** evidence. But individuals can still be sometimes swayed by this kind of faulty logic. For instance, consider the following example of faulty inductive reasoning based on flawed connections between facts.

> **First premise:** Some new immigrant neighbors moved into my neighborhood a year ago.
> **Second premise:** In the last year, there has been an increase in robberies in the neighborhood.
> **Conclusion:** Foreign people are thieves.

From this kind of example, you can see that inductive reasoning can sometimes appear to be logical, but still be invalid, untrue, and harmful.

Deductive reasoning can also lead to conclusions that are logical but not true. This is due to the fact that the premises, or statements of fact, in deductive reasoning can be used in different ways to arrive at different conclusions. Consider the following classical example:

Major premise: All dogs <u>need sleep</u>.
Minor premise: Jimmy <u>needs sleep</u>.
Conclusion: Jimmy is a dog.

If you have a pet terrier named Jimmy, you may not have a problem with this. But your friend Jimmy may question it. Now consider an alternative way of determining Jimmy's species and need for sleep:

Major premise: <u>All dogs</u> need sleep.
Minor premise: Jimmy <u>is a dog</u>.
Conclusion: Jimmy needs sleep.

You will have noticed that some of the words in the premises above have been underlined. That is to point out that major premises have two parts, and that minor premises can refer back to either one of these parts. The first part of the major premise is the ***subject*** of the statement ("All dogs," in the above examples). It is underlined in the second example. The second part of the major premise is the ***predicate*** of the statement ("need sleep," in the above examples). It is underlined in the first example.

Notice that trouble begins when the ***minor premise***, or the second statement, refers to the ***predicate*** part of the major premise. This occurs in the first example, in which your friend Jimmy unwittingly became a dog. Yet in the second example, the ***minor premise*** refers back to the ***subject*** part of the ***major premise***. This leads to more valid reasoning, and definitely states that the Jimmy in question is, in this instance, a dog.

There are many more complexities and variations within the study of logic. This exercise is given to illustrate that reasoning can be faulty, and that the exact point at which it fails can be identified through the science of logic. As a critical reader, you may be able to pinpoint where logic becomes weak through a basic understanding of logic and a careful reading of the text.

Judgment

At some point, a careful reading and critical examination of any text, including your SAT essay prompt and assignment, should lead you to a **judgment** of the text and of the ideas in it. You may decide

- that an author's ideas are innovative, insightful, well supported, and comprehensive
- that the author is well qualified to write about the subject matter
- that the author's ideas are well presented, but that the author failed to take a particular aspect of the argument into consideration
- that the main idea of the text is vague and that the supporting ideas are arbitrary
- that the perspective of the author is biased, based on the author's affiliation
- that the author is not qualified to write as an authority on the subject
- that the author's argument is based on emotion rather than reason.

You may also decide that several of the above judgments are true, as well as possible others. All of them are valid if you can support them with evidence from the text and from research or experience. These judgments form the basis of your response to the text. A critical reader always has a response, even if it is simply agreement. When this response is expressed in a clear statement, you have the beginning of a thesis for a critical essay on the text.

Forming an Argument

Forming an **argument** for a critical essay is accomplished when you go through the processes listed above in reading a text. Once you have read carefully, asked questions, researched further, considered the **logic**, **voice**, and **tone** of the author, and formed your judgement, you are ready to write your argument. Writing your argument begins with articulating your main idea clearly. All the steps in writing a persuasive essay are discussed in chapter 4. For now, articulating your main idea, based on your careful reading of the text, is a solid beginning. Imagine you have read an article about the oppression of individual freedoms imposed by the Patriot Act of the United States. You have looked into the 5 Ws and H of the author and the publisher, and you have carefully read the article for clear ideas, valid reasoning, and strong evidence. Finally, you have made a judgement that the article is innovative, sound, and well-supported, but that it has failed to take into consideration some aspects of the argument.

Once you have made your judgment, write down your argument in one sentence, if possible. It may look something like this: "I believe that the Patriot Act of the United States diminishes personal freedoms of U.S. citizens, but that a successful democracy must be a balance between personal freedoms and general good."

With a clear argument articulated in words, you can collect your supporting ideas, along with evidence to back up each. First you might reread the original text to find specific points you want to argue against. List those points, then list ideas from your own experience, from reasoning, and from research and observation.

Finally, write another single sentence which sums up your conclusion. It may look something like "The general welfare of a nation rests on a balance informed by a treasuring of freedom and safety and a willingness to forego some minor privileges to achieve that state."

Critical thinking has led to a clear and well considered argument and outline for a critical response to your reading. The next chapter will take you through the specific steps of producing an effective opinion essay.

Practice 3: Forming an Argument

Read the following quotes and assignment, then form a one-sentence statement of an argument you might reach from them.

The grand maxim on which civil and political society in the United States rests is that Providence has given to every human being the degree of reason necessary to direct himself in the affairs which interest him exclusively.

– French historian Alexis de Toqueville (1805 – 1859)

How selfish man may be supposed, there are evidently some principles in his nature, which interest him in the fortune of others, and render their happiness necessary to him, though he derives nothing from it except the pleasure of seeing it.

– Scottish economist Adam Smith (1723 – 1790)

Assignment: Do human beings have a basic interest in the good fortunes of others, or do they care only for what affects them personally? Plan and write an essay that develops your point of view. Support your position with reasoning and examples taken from your reading, studies, experience, or observations.

Chapter 3 Review

Answer the following questions by referring back to the information in the chapter. Use a separate sheet of paper to write your answers.

1. What tool that you can hold in your hand is helpful in the process of critical thinking?
2. What kind of words should one underline when carefully reading any text?
3. What are the 8 characteristics of critical thinking discussed in this chapter?
4. Why are the "5 Ws and H" an important step in critical thinking?
5. What qualities should a critical reader look for in an author's evidence?
6. Why is open-mindedness important in critical thinking, even if a reader's mind is not ultimately changed by reading a text?
7. What are the technical terms for the two parts of a major premise in deductive reasoning? What parts of a sentence do these two term describe?
8. List five possible conclusions a reader might reach from critically examining a text.

Chapter 4
Writing the Opinion Essay

What can you do in 25 minutes? You can bake one pan of brownies for friends, you can watch one Simpson's episode on DVD, or you can drive 25 miles at 60 miles per hour.

Twenty-five minutes. This is the amount of time you have to write one essay in rough draft form for the SAT Essay section. Since this is a rough draft essay, the reader will be looking first for appropriate supporting ideas and for the essay to make a clear statement of opinion. At the end of this chapter you will find the section **"Student Resources: Web Sites and Books."** There are several excellent sites and texts which cover the writing topics you may want to practice.

Below is a list of topics which will be covered in this chapter. These topics will help you to create an essay with appropriate supporting ideas and a clear opinion. You will have already seen most of these topics in your study of language arts, but consider this a look back in order to look ahead at the SAT essay.

Chapter Topic List

PREWRITING

- Opinion: Form One and Keep It Constant
- Analyze the Prompt
- Planning Your Essay

WRITING

- Write an Introduction that Grabs Attention
- Write Supporting Body Paragraphs
- Write a Strong Conclusion

POST-WRITING

- Scanning Your Essay (If Time Allows)
- Comparing Sample Essays as Practice

PREWRITING

Prewriting is the most important step you take in writing any essay. Prewriting involves a careful reading of the prompt, forming your opinion, analyzing the prompt, and planning out the essay.

Keep in mind that prewriting will begin only when the test is officially begun, as prewriting is part of the timed writing session. During the test, you will want to spend only about five minutes on these prewriting steps.

OPINION: FORM ONE AND KEEP IT CONSTANT

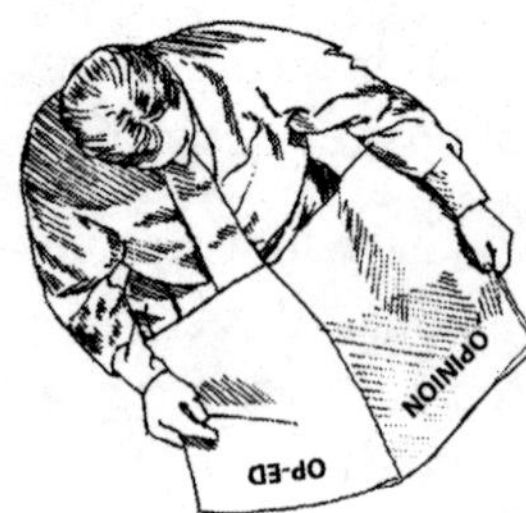

An **opinion** is a judgment or a belief about a person, place, object, or idea. You probably hear opinions all the time. Most of these are simple comparisons, such as "Our team is the best!" "This city is the worst!" "Our school dance sounds so lame!" For the SAT essay, you will be asked to form an opinion about an issue. It does not matter what your opinion is, but you must form one quickly. Your opinion will need supporting statements and evidence. (How to integrate ideas and experiences and prior knowledge into your essay is discussed in **Chapter 3: Critical Thinking**.)

NOTE: There is danger here. As you write your opinion essay, you may find your opinion shifting to another viewpoint. Be strong! Use the essays in this book as practice in keeping your opinion constant. Start with one strong opinion and hold it all the way through.

ANALYZE THE PROMPT

The SAT Test essay prompt is formatted in two parts:

- a writing prompt for a topic or issue, presented in a short paragraph, and
- an assignment which has instructions detailing what elements to include in your essay.

After carefully reading the prompt and assignment once, you will have formed your opinion. Scanning the assignment again may help focus your thoughts, can be done quickly, and will help to start your planning with a specific direction in mind.

The following prompt and assignment are modeled after the SAT Test format in both structure and the type of topics presented. Read this sample to familiarize yourself with the format and language.

Writing Prompt

Think carefully about the issue described in the excerpt below and about the assignment that follows it.

> *Einstein's space is no closer to reality than Van Gogh's sky. The glory of science is not in truth more absolute than the truth of Bach or Tolstoy, but in the act of creation itself. The scientist's discoveries impose his own order on chaos, as the composer or painter imposes his; an order that always refers to limited aspects of reality and is based on the observer's frame of reference.*
>
> – *Quoting Arthur Koestler (Hungarian-born British writer)*

Assignment: What is your opinion on the claim that science is not an absolute truth, but is, instead, an art which depends on a vision of truth? Plan and write an essay in which you develop your point of view (opinion) on the issue. Support your opinion with reasons and evidence brought from your own experience, your studies, or from your observations.

You may want to reread the prompt and then scan the assignment. If you write your essay off topic, remember, it will AUTOMATICALLY be scored as a ZERO.

The topic paragraph and the assignment are repeated below. This time, key words are **bolded** in the assignment. Look over the material and think about the words which have been bolded.

Writing Prompt

> *Einstein's space is no closer to reality than Van Gogh's sky. The glory of science is not in truth more absolute than the truth of Bach or Tolstoy, but in the act of creation itself. The scientist's discoveries impose his own order on chaos, as the composer or painter imposes his; an order that always refers to limited aspects of reality and is based on the observer's frame of reference.*
>
> – *Quoting Arthur Koestler (Hungarian-born British writer)*

Assignment: What is **your opinion** on the claim that **science** is **not** an **absolute truth, but** is, rather, **an art** which depends on a **vision of truth. Plan and write** an essay in which you develop **your point of view** (opinion) on the **issue. Support** your opinion with **reasons and evidence** brought from your own **experience**, your **studies**, or from your **observations.**

For your SAT essay, the topic in the prompt will be different but the assignment will be similar. All assignments for the SAT will require you to state your opinion with support. This particular example asks for your opinion on science and truth. It requires you to both plan and write an essay which supports your opinion, in the form of **experience**, **studies**, or **observations**.

Planning Your Essay

Notice that the assignment asks you to "**Plan** and write an essay . . ."

For a 25-minute rough draft essay, the best **planning** is known as "**The Quick & Messy Outline.**" We recommend that you budget a short **5 minutes** to plan, sketching a brief outline on the test booklet page with the prompt and the assignment. You may glance back to the assignment once you have started on the essay just to check that you are on topic, but you should do that only once, if at all.

The following outline was created in the 5-minute time limit. It shows the writer's opinion about the issue and enough ways to support it in order to create a three to five paragraph essay.

NOTE: Since organization is part of the writing skills assessed in the SAT essay, we recommend that you plan on writing at least three paragraphs. A total of four or five paragraphs would be even better. The SAT essay **does not** have to be written in the four-to-five-paragraph format, yet that is a common method and is something graders are comfortable with reading — this is the KISS principle at work — Keep It Simple, Student.

5-minute Quick & Messy Outline for SAT Essay

1. Main Idea — Science is not absolute truth — changes with time periods and new discoveries disproving old + Poe's poem To Science

2. Paleontology - — dinosaurs change w/ fashion and worldview — dumb and slow / now fast and smart

3. medicine - — aspirin from willow tree not known how it works and seen as common— now: miracle drug! New drug fiascos

4. Life: Birth and death — - standards for label- viable person in womb/ when is a person determined to be dead-Has changed

Conclusion — Science not truth- changes with time

The outline lacks end punctuation; it has run-ons, contractions, dashes and the occasional misspelling. This is a good example of the quick & messy 3 - 5 minute outline. Notice, too, that all the examples are well-known to most people, and there are thousands of other arguments both for and against this opinion. This essay could be written from personal experience or observations as well.

Practice 1: Prewriting

Read each of the following three prompts. Form an opinion, analyze the prompts, and then on your own paper, write a 5-minute Quick & Messy Outline. Use whatever is fastest and most comfortable for you.

Writing Prompt 1

A foolish consistency is the hobgoblin of little minds, adored by little statesmen and philosophers and divines. With consistency a great soul has simply nothing to do. He may as well concern himself with his shadow on the wall. Speak what you think now in hard words, and to-morrow speak what to-morrow thinks in hard words again, though it contradict every thing you said to-day.

Excerpt from Ralph Waldo Emerson's Self-Reliance (1841)

Assignment: What is your opinion about the wisdom of being consistent or the flexibility of being inconsistent? Plan and write an essay in which you develop your point of view (opinion) on the issue. Support your opinion with reasons and evidence brought from your own experience, your studies, or from your observations.

Writing Prompt 2

He covered page after page with wild words of sorrow and wilder words of pain. There is a luxury in self-reproach. When we blame ourselves, we feel that no one else has a right to blame us. It is the confession, not the priest that gives us absolution.

Excerpt from Oscar Wilde's The Picture of Dorian Gray

Assignment: Do people blame themselves and apologize to make themselves feel better or to make others feel better? Plan and write an essay in which you develop your point of view (opinion) on the issue. Support your opinion with reasons and evidence brought from your own experience, your studies, or from your observations.

Writing Prompt 3

Temptation: Do people experience this influence in different ways? C. S. Lewis wrote that only people who try to resist temptation know how strong it can be. He says that people who give into temptation immediately never feel its real pull; that is the difference between good people and bad people.

Paraphrase of C. S. Lewis

Assignment: Could some people feel the full strength of temptation immediately in the first moments, while "better people" have a resistance to temptation built into their personalities? What is your view on this question? Plan and write an essay in which you develop your point of view (opinion) on the issue. Support your opinion with reasons and evidence brought from your own experience, your studies, or from your observations.

NOTE: Keep a portfolio of all your work for the practices in this chapter. This work will be built upon in later practices.

WRITING

After planning the essay, your time to write a rough draft is down to only 20 minutes! Not surprisingly, this second phase of the writing process takes a great amount of concentration or focus. Follow the instructions given by the test proctor (instructor) using only the lined paper of the *answer booklet* for your writing. You may want to take a deep breath and exhale slowly as you begin.

Remember:

- You now have 20 minutes
- Focus on holding to one opinion
- Follow your outline as closely as possible

WRITE AN ATTENTION-GETTING INTRODUCTION

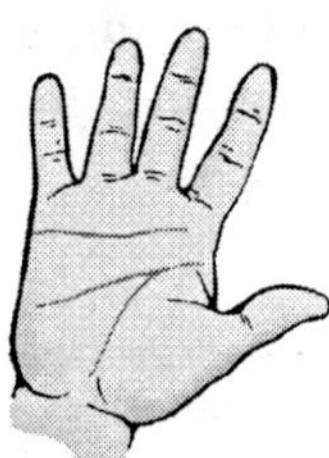

Treat this as a "hello" to the reader and know that this is the first impression your reader will have of you. The essay for the SAT will be an opinion essay. Not all of the different forms of introduction will work with that type of essay. Also, with the 20-minute time limit, you will want to make this quick.

The **introduction** is the first paragraph of your essay. It may be shorter than the body paragraphs or just a little longer, but it serves an important purpose. It tells readers where you are going and invites them along. It should catch the readers' interest and clearly state the thesis of the essay. The introduction may also inform readers of the order of support for the thesis.

You have probably have seen stores that attract customers by placing a huge, fluorescent-colored sign outside, advertising an incredible sale. This approach to sales is somewhat similar to how you want to lead readers into your essay, catching their attention and leading in. A simple way to build an introduction is by using the following three components: **lead**, **tie-in**, and **thesis**.

LEAD

Sometimes you can start your essay by stating its thesis, but often that type of beginning is too abrupt. You need to grab the reader's attention first, and make him want to read on. You can do this with the first sentence, called a **lead**. The lead may be one of the following:

- Statement of position on the topic
- Problem or riddle
- Surprising statistic or fact
- Catchy remark
- Question
- Historical review
- General, thought-provoking statement
- Famous person

Tie-In

Once you have captured the readers' attention with your lead, you need to draw their attention to the thesis of your essay. You need to consider the audience, the topic of your essay, your point of view, and your personal preference in developing a creative link between the lead and statement of your thesis.

Thesis

The first paragraph is a good place to state the thesis because it lets the reader know the topic of the essay, your position on the topic, and how you are going to order your supporting points.

Different Types of Introductions

Below, you will find examples of introductions that use different types of leads followed by a tie-in and a statement of the thesis. The first example is labeled for you. For the other examples, circle the lead, [bracket] the tie-in, and underline the statement of the thesis.

State Your Position on the Topic

> *Science does not have the absolute truth formulated for all eternity.* Some may think scientific measurements and graphs and hypotheses cover any uncertainties. [But scientific ideas and formulas and definitions change apace with the cycles of the sun and moon.] As for proof of this theory, the following are only three examples out of many showing "science" in the throes of change occurring even today: dinosaurs, aspirin, and the question of what is life and what is death.

Here, the writer's position is stated directly and emphatically in the first line. This emphatic declaration is an attention-getter and invites discussion. The author briefly comments on a possible objection to the topic sentence and then states the thesis in the last sentence of this brief introduction.

Problem or Riddle

> Here's a riddle: What is the greatest defender, yet the greatest threat to Truth? Give up? For every age, Science pronounces Truth and denies any possible deviation. Can we believe this, or can we look beyond the rhetoric of scientists? We can look past and beyond for the proof that science is in constant flux. From the way dinosaurs behaved, the use of aspirin, to the question of the beginning of life and the endings of death, Science has said it has absolute Truth, even though it changes with time and fashion.

Unlike the introduction that states your purpose right off, the "riddle" introduction holds back information while teasing the reader to guess what it might be. This writer even labeled the first line as a riddle — delaying the opening and setting up an expectation in the reader. Notice how this introduction gives examples that support the thesis.

Surprising Statistic or Fact

Throughout the centuries, people have been routinely buried alive based on the changing definition of death. Today, scientists and doctors have pushed back the veil of death by the use of sophisticated brain scans, changing what we understand of life and death. Science, which seems so stable and all knowing, is actually inconsistent and unknowing as far as holding absolute knowledge or truth. We can forgive science for this failing as long as it recognizes the same. Life and death are not the only scientific inconsistencies; there are many others, including the behavior of dinosaurs and the properties of aspirin. Science touches our lives in countless ways, but we need to remind ourselves that it is not infallible.

A statistic or fact is only surprising if it contradicts common beliefs or perceptions. Regarding burying people alive, that is perceived as something which happens only in science fiction or gothic novels. What readers may not understand is that with sophisticated equipment, people who present every aspect of being dead may have minimal brain function as opposed to having no function at all. In the past, they would have been pronounced dead and then buried. This fact will catch the attention of readers and make them want to continue reading.

Question

What do you expect from science? Do you expect all answers to all things for all times? If so, disappointment is in your future. The one true fact scientists have discovered is that everything changes, even scientific truths. There are many scientific "truths" which have been altered over time, for example the behavior of dinosaurs, the benefits of aspirin, and the definitions of life and death. In your lifetime you will most likely see other scientific truths debunked and new truths take their place — for a while.

Beginning an essay with a question or two automatically engages readers and makes them start thinking. It also creates curiosity about how you will answer the question, making the readers wonder if you will agree or disagree. In the example above, notice that the answer the author gives is rather blunt.

Quotation

"There are three kinds of lies: lies, dang lies, and statistics." Statistics, meaning numbers, and the lies — even if inadvertent — result from different interpretations of numbers. Science interprets numbers; its truth is generated by numerical measurements and evaluations. But scientific truth can lie. Interpretations of the numbers may be colored by what scientists expect to find, hope to find, or must find. Countless examples of scientific truth gone wrong exist, including dinosaur behavior, the value of aspirin, and the measurement of life and death. Numbers and their lies need a reality check.

Any quote that you can remember and easily relate to your topic will make a good lead for your introduction. This may be difficult — to have an appropriate quote memorized — but you may be surprised at what you can think of when a prompt nudges or prods your memory.

Famous Person

In the past two decades, our world has been speeding towards a future only dreamt of in the realm of science fiction writers, such as Jules Verne, Edgar Allen Poe, H. G. Wells, Isaac Asimov, and Ursula K. Le Guin. Of these writers, Poe is the one who displays an overt ambivalence to the machinations of science. He wrote a sonnet chiding science for eliminating, bit by bit, the mystery and majesty of the natural world. With our society ever accelerating towards the future, science seems to be doubling back on itself. Scientific thought has seldom been absolute truth, even though scientists imply that it is always so. There are myriad examples of scientific thought being rethought: the life of dinosaurs, the medical properties of aspirin, and the parameters of life and death.

Using the name of a famous person or people and tying them into the essay's general topic is a way to attract readers' attention. Usually people grant authority to the famous and eagerly read their opinions. Using this lead will often draw readers into the introduction and will bring them to your thesis. In this example, the essay writer mentions several science fiction writers and then emphasizes the opinion of Poe, who held a similar opinion to the one being expressed in the essay.

Practice 2: Attention-Getting Introductions

For this practice, look back to the three prompts given in Practice 1. For each of the prompts, form an opinion and write an attention-getting introduction. For each of the prompts, use a different type of introduction. Use the choices given for introductions in the section on leads. Model your introductions on the examples from the section "**Different Types of Introductions.**"

After writing the three introductions, trade your three with a classmate's and read each other's as a peer review. Use specific comments if you have suggestions for a change. Remember you will learn from your classmates' writing as they learn from yours. You may seek feedback on your writing in your school or your home: language arts teachers, counselors, or parents. It is best if you can get feedback from a person who has a good instinct for clear writing.

NOTE: Keep a portfolio of all your work for the practices in this chapter. This work will be built upon in later practices.

Write Supporting Body Paragraphs

Now that you have introduced yourself and your essay by writing a focused introduction, including your opinion and some supporting topics, you are ready to write the body paragraphs. Body paragraphs provide the details and examples which support the opinion stated in the introduction. When you write your body paragraphs, you will want to follow your outline and keep a consistent opinion.

You may want to refer back to **Chapter 1: Writing Paragraphs** for general information on composing well-structured paragraphs, the appropriate number range of sentences in a paragraph, and the transitions needed for the clarity and logical flow between each paragraph.

The following body paragraphs are written for the sample introduction using the quotation lead.

Quotation

"There are three kinds of lies: lies, dang lies, and statistics." Statistics, meaning numbers, and the lies — even if inadvertent — result from different interpretations of numbers. Science interprets numbers; its truth is generated by numerical measurements and evaluations. Scientific truth can lie. Interpretations of the numbers may be colored by what scientists expect to find — hope to find — or must find. Countless examples of scientific truth gone wrong exist, including dinosaur behavior, the value of aspirin, and the measurement of life and death. Numbers and their lies need a reality check.

The following three body paragraphs are in rough draft form. With the introductory paragraph and conclusion, this will make the sample essay five paragraphs long. You will want to organize your essay as between three and five paragraphs in length.

Body Paragraphs

Historical reality hit hard in the 1800s when dinosaur fossils were discovered; the study of these "thunder lizards," was marred by measurements and wild postulations. The first paleontologists assured an awestruck public that these creatures were too "dumb" to survive alongside *Homo sapiens*. Brain cavity measurements led scientists to say that dinosaur brains were walnut-sized, too small to control enormous bodies. Even the tyrannosaurs rex was portrayed as a slow giant whose tiny forearms waved ineffectively under deadly jaws. In the past decade, this view has spun 180 degrees. Scientists who have measured the stride of dinosaurs and discovered nests, report that dinosaurs were related to birds, warm-blooded, and intelligent enough to have social structures. They say dinosaurs were wiped out, not by ignorance, but by a cataclysmic event; are you people listening? The scientific truth about dinosaurs changed for real, but maybe not forever.

Another elusive truth is the true nature of aspirin. The ubiquitous aspirin tablet was heralded as a miracle cure, then dismissed as mundane, almost dangerous, and is now, again, hailed as a miracle. What is the truth? Doctors first developed aspirin from willow bark extract. They prescribed aspirin for reducing tissue swelling, cooling fevers, relieving headaches, and soothing other pains. Sounds miraculous, but in the brave new world of synthetic drugs, scientists developed other medicines thought safer and more effective. In the past decade, during a rush to natural and herbal remedies, scientists saw newer drugs cause serious side effects. They have since praised aspirin for its relative safety and ability to reduce the severity of heart attacks. Once again, scientific truth changes with fashion and new information.

The parameters of life and death: What truths have changed more with cultural opinion and scientific fact? None. Before the 1900s, life was said to begin when birth took place. Scientific revelations about procreation and life in the mother's womb caused definition changes. Life is now said to begin when an egg is fertilized. Scientific study then begat changes in how life is created: in-vitro clones and frozen eggs all change scientific truths about where and how life begins. For that matter, scientists have changed the definition and boundaries of death. New methods for keeping the body alive, in the news and in the hospitals, keep death a complex slippery concept. Cryogenics, the science of keeping bodies frozen until reviving to new cures has made the true point of death more uncertain than ever.

This sample essay uses common knowledge within the culture as well as material from science classes for supporting details. There are many other supporting topics which could have been used to support the opinion: theories about the Big Bang, Artificial Intelligence discoveries, new information from space, string theory, and new ideas from sub-atomic theory. Or you may write about experiences in your life which have run counter to scientific truth, describing them and then connecting them to the topic. Whatever support you choose, use the first few minutes in the writing session to outline your ideas and form an opinion — after that, you just write what you think, using your detailed support.

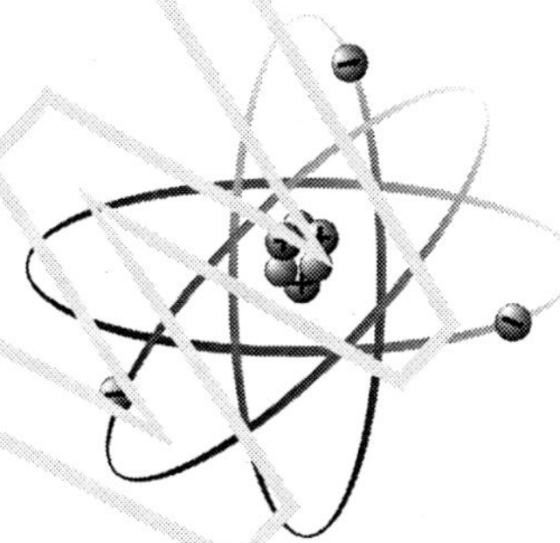

Practice 3: Analyzing Body Paragraphs

Reread the sample essay, both introduction and body paragraphs from the preceding sections. Then underline the topic sentences in each paragraph, circle transitional words or phrases, and bracket [ ] the supporting details given in each paragraph.

"There are three kinds of lies: lies, dang lies, and statistics." Statistics, meaning numbers, and the lies — even if inadvertent — result from different interpretations of numbers. Science interprets numbers; its truth is generated by numerical measurements and evaluations. Scientific truth can lie. Interpretations of the numbers may be colored by what scientists expect to find, or hope to find, or must find. Countless examples of scientific truth gone wrong exist, including dinosaur behavior, the value of aspirin, and the measurement of life and death. Numbers and their lies need a reality check.

Historical reality hit hard in the 1800s when dinosaur fossils were discovered; the study of these "terrible lizards," cold-blooded dinosaurs, was marred by measurements and wild postulations. The first paleontologists assured an awestruck public that these creatures were too "dumb" to survive alongside *Homo sapiens*. Brain cavity measurements led scientists to say that dinosaur brains were walnut-sized. They asserted this was too small to control enormous bodies. Even the tyrannosaurus rex was portrayed as a slow giant whose tiny forearms waved ineffectively under deadly jaws. In the past decade, this view has turned 180 degrees. Scientists who have measured the stride of dinosaurs, and discovered nests, and studied bone structure, report that dinosaurs were related to birds, warm-blooded, and intelligent enough to have social structures. They say dinosaurs were wiped out, not by ignorance, but by a cataclysmic event; are you people listening? The scientific truth about dinosaurs changed for real, but maybe not forever.

Another elusive truth is the true nature of aspirin. The ubiquitous aspirin tablet was heralded as a miracle cure, then dismissed as mundane, almost dangerous, and is now, again, hailed as a miracle. What is the truth? Doctors first developed aspirin from willow bark extract. They prescribed aspirin for reducing tissue swelling, cooling fevers, relieving headaches, and soothing other pains. Sounds miraculous, but in the brave new world of synthetic drugs, scientists developed other medicines thought safer and more effective. In the past decade, during a rush to natural and herbal remedies, scientists saw newer drugs cause serious side effects. They have since praised aspirin for its relative safety and ability to reduce the severity of heart attacks. Once again, scientific truth changes with fashion and new information.

The parameters of life and death: What truths have changed more with cultural opinion and scientific fact? None. Before the 1900s, life was said to begin when birth took place. Scientific revelations about procreation and life in the mother's womb caused definition changes. Life is now said to begin when an egg is fertilized. Scientific study then begat changes in how life is created: in-vitro, clones, and frozen eggs all change scientific truths about where and how life begins. For that matter, scientists have changed the definition and boundaries of death. New methods for keeping the body alive, in the news and in the hospitals, keep death a complex slippery concept. Cryogenics, the science of keeping bodies frozen until reviving to new cures has made the true point of death more uncertain than ever.

Practice 4: Writing Body Paragraphs

For this practice, look again at the three prompts given in Practice 1. Choose one of the prompts. Using the introduction you developed in the previous practice, add supporting body paragraphs. Write two to three of these while you check on your progress — make sure you stay focused on one opinion.

After writing your body paragraphs, trade them with a classmate and read each other's as a peer review. Use specific comments if you have suggestions for a change, using positive statements. Then show your Language Arts teacher your draft for more feedback.

NOTE: Keep a portfolio of all your work for the practices in this chapter. You will revise this work in later practices.

Write a Strong Conclusion

If you think of your essay as a race, with the thesis statement the starting gate and the body paragraphs the track and course, the conclusion is the finish line. Writing a conclusion that's strong, focused, and compelling is the difference between bounding through the victory tape and staggering along, wheezing for breath.

You want to restate your original opinion (from the introduction) but not in the same words, include a brisk summary of your main points, and wrap everything up with a focused, succinct closing. A closer for the paragraphs in the preceding section might look like this:

> So what do the lessons of ancient dynamic dinosaurs, modern medicine's new old miracle drug, and the shifting boundaries of life and death teach us? They all teach us that scientific discovery and subsequent scientific "truths" cannot be lined up like colorful wooden counting beads — equaling out to the secrets of life. Instead, the discoveries may be understood as the gentle clacking sounds the counting beads make — answered by questioning and new discoveries — always seeking the changes, scientific and cultural, inherent in this life.

Notice that this conclusion first makes a quick summary of the essay's main points, and then restates the opinion using the image of counting beads. This image reflects the introduction's idea of numbers being misleading in the pursuit of truth. The wooden counting beads, while a new image, are not part of a new idea. You will want to avoid adding new information to your conclusion, but it is fine to add punch to your final clinching statement by using a vivid image to communicate your opinion. You will have a clincher of a conclusion.

Practice 5: Writing Conclusions

Go back to the outlines you wrote for Practice 1 and the introductions you wrote for Practice 2. Take the two you have not used for the body paragraphs and the conclusion practices, and write a conclusion for each. Look carefully at your outlines and your introductions for the supporting details and opinions you will need to develop a conclusion for each. As a guide, reread the sample conclusion on science and truth.

After you have completed your two conclusions, trade them with a classmate for peer review or ask for feedback from your teacher.

Practice 6: A Strong Conclusion

For this practice, look back to the introduction and body paragraphs you developed in Practice 4. Using these two essay sections, write a concluding paragraph.

After writing your body paragraphs, trade them with a classmate and read each other's as a peer review. Use specific comments if you have suggestions for a change, using positive statements.

NOTE: Keep a portfolio of all your work for the practices in this chapter. This work will be revisited in later practices.

POST-WRITING

The 25 minutes you began this essay with are almost gone. Let's say that you are down to 2 minutes and 17 seconds remaining for this session of the SAT exam. What do you do now?

If you have time remaining, there are some editing fixes you could make quickly. In 2 minutes and 17 seconds or even in just a few seconds, you could scan your essay for misspellings, stray punctuation errors, or shifting tenses and point of view. After enough practice, you will know your individual tendencies when writing an essay. Understand what your tendencies are and scan for those in the time you have remaining, if any.

When you have zero time, put that yellow #2 pencil down and unwind.

Student Resources: Web Sites and Books

Writing Essays

http://owl.english.purdue.edu/

This site is titled the Purdue On-line Writing Center. The university's resources are the bedrock of the site. There are numerous printable hand-outs and lessons. The sections on writing paragraphs and essays will be a valuable tool for students who enjoy working on-line.

http://grammar.ccc.commnet.edu/grammar

The Guide to Grammar and Writing is an excellent starting place for anyone who needs to practice from the sentence level to a full research paper. There are quizzes, lists of writing devices, and a full discussion of point of view. It also offers numerous links to other Web sites.

http://www.essaypunch.com

Essay Punch, a free service of Merit Software, walks users through each step of the essay writing process, providing advice and counseling for prewriting brainstorming tips to revising concluding sentences. The pages are easy to use, written on a level easily accessible to a broad audience, and organized with plenty of cross-referencing.

Books

Martha E. Campbell. Focus: From Paragraph to Essay. Upper Saddle River, NJ: Prentiss Hall, 1996.

A fine practical and easy to read text that integrates composition and grammar concepts.

Victor Pellegrino. A Writer's Guide to Using Eight Methods of Transition. Wailuku: Maui Arthoughts Company, 1993.

Presents itself as a brief but enlightening guide—an invaluable reference tool that helps writers choose the best transitional words and expressions for a context. The author provides a close look at how to create connections in sentences and paragraphs.

Chapter 4 Review

A. Read the following rough draft essay. After reading, analyze the essay for elements practiced in this chapter and some from previous chapters. Write your comments on a separate sheet of paper. Use the following questions to frame your analysis:

Writing Prompt

> *Many years ago the great British explorer George Mallory, who was to die on Mount Everest, was asked why he wanted to climb it. He said "Because it is there." Well, space is there, and we're going to climb it, and the moon and the planets are there, and new hopes for knowledge and peace are there.*
>
> *President John F. Kennedy, speech, 1962*
>
> **Assignment:** Do you agree with the idea that people need to push beyond existing boundaries to find knowledge and peace? Or do you think that knowledge and peace can be found wherever it is sought? Plan and write an essay in which you develop your point of view (opinion) on the issue. Support your opinion with reasons and evidence brought from your own experience, studies, or observations.

Essay

As President Kennedy implied, knowledge and peace seem to be ideals best looked for somewhere over the rainbow or beyond. Knowledge found here on earth often takes the form of learning new devious technologies to destroy and corrupt social fabrics and societies. Advantages in physics in the 1940s were turned to mass destruction by the atomic bomb. Peace on this earth is so fleeting and rare, that even in utopias no peace could last. What turns knowledge to the evil side and twists yearnings for peace into power struggles? Human nature may be that volaitile flash point. Looking for knowledge and peace must then be found in places so alien that human nature may be transcended.

Human nature is an inquisitive beast, always grasping at the mysterious and misunderstood. Albert Einstein, the gentle scientist who pondered the cosmos in his woolen socks, supported the construction of the atomic bomb until, realizing the mistake of unleashing such power, asked President Truman not to use nuclear weapons against Japan. But in wartime the temptation of such power was irresistible, and Truman ordered the nuclear attacks on Hiroshima and Nagasaki. Again, human nature struggled to combat fears — the fear of defeat, the fear of losing millions more men in war — by creating something more terrifying than anything else before it using newfound language.

Utopias have risen and fallen throughout the span of history in almost all countries. Utopias are defined as unworldly places of perfect peace on earth. None of them have survived for more than a few decades — most collapsing quickly under the weight of rivalry, jealousy and the seductions of power. Even in our schools where the ideal is to have a peaceful coexistence of peer groups, we always have human nature to contend with. The book *Lord of the Flies* is a good example of a paradise being lost to the struggle for power. Spaceship crews are selected for their good natures and "playing well with others." I guess when your life depends on getting along it's a totally different thing than losing TV time.

Knowledge and peace have been looked for through out the ages and found in micro-seconds and then lost again. President Kennedy may have been right, saying that knowledge and peace are out there to be discovered — but it may be in an altarnate universe or on a celestial plane where human nature may be transformed that they be truly found.

1. Is there a strong opinion stated in the introduction? Give support for your response.
2. Is the opinion consistent through the essay? Give support for your response.
3. What person is used in the essay?
4. Is the use of person consistent? Give support for your response.
5. Is the introduction effective in getting the reader's attention? Explain how.
6. Do the body paragraphs fully support the ideas stated in the introduction?
7. Does the essay reach a logical, effective conclusion that clinches the essay's point? Give reasons for your response.
8. Is the rough draft mostly free of spelling, grammar, and punctuation errors?

B. Read the following two quotations and accompanying assignments. Choose one and write an outline and then an essay, following the assignment directions. For this essay, use the 25 minute time frame. Also, be sure to use a consistent opinion and point of view. Remember also to write body paragraphs which support your opinion logically and write a conclusion which restates the introduction, but with an attitude.

Writing Prompt 1

"I heartily accept the motto, "That government is best which governs least"; and I should like to see it acted up to more rapidly and systematically. Carried out, it finally amounts to this, which also I believe — "That government is best which governs not at all"; and when men are prepared for it, that will be the kind of government which they will have.

Thoreau, Civil Disobedience

Assignment: Remember Thoreau is the writer who encouraged his fellow Americans to embrace a philosophy of simplicity. Do you agree or disagree that people prefer and deserve a government which governs simply (least) or not at all? Plan and write an essay in which you develop your point of view (opinion) on the issue. Support your opinion with reasons and evidence brought from your own experience, studies, or observations.

Writing Prompt 2

But I do not believe it is man's destiny to compress this once boundless earth into a small neighborhood, the better to destroy it. Nor do I believe it is in the nature of man to strike eternally at the image of himself, and therefore of God. I profoundly believe that there is on this horizon, as yet only dimly perceived, a new dawn of conscience. .[people] will make themselves known to one another by their similarities rather than by their differences...The significance of a smaller world...will be the triumph of the heartbeat over the drumbeat.

Adlai Stevenson, speech (24th October, 1952)

Assignment: Adlai Stevenson, a Democrat who ran for president in the 1950s, gave this speech long before the term "Global Village" was coined. Is it your opinion that the perceived shrinking of our world is fostering understanding and peace, or is it provoking its opposite — intolerance and war? Plan and write an essay in which you develop your point of view (opinion) on the issue. Support your opinion with reasons and evidence brought from your own experience, studies, or observations.

NOTE: Keep this essay in the portfolio of your practice work. You will be using this essay in **Chapter 9: Neophyte's Guide to Scoring SAT Essays.**

Chapter 5
The Write Stuff: Avoiding Errors

Unfortunately, avoiding writing errors is not like dodging alien spacecraft in a video game. There's no safe place to hide or a smart strategy for escaping the issue. Writing only short simple sentences is a red flag that tells readers that the writer lacks basic skills. The SAT essay, though written in rough draft form, needs to demonstrate the writer's basic knowledge of writing skills.

The readers for the SAT essay will be looking first at ideas and a logical progression of opinion, but they will down score an essay with numerous faults in sentence formation and the mechanics of standardized English. So how to avoid errors when writing for the SAT? Practice writing with correct grammar, usage, and mechanics.

TIP

Write it right the first time through.

The best way to practice writing your essay right the first time is to take an honest look at your writing skills, deciding which skills are strong and which ones need strengthening. Armed with that information, you can target specific areas for improvement.

Proofreading your essays will reveal the type of errors that show up in your writing. This chapter will give you a quick look at how to check your essays for errors in grammar, spelling, capitalization, and punctuation, as well as for repeated or omitted words.

TIP

Practice proofreading quickly and with an eye to a pattern of errors, if any.

Readers will look to your rough draft essay to determine your knowledge of standardized English through grammar and usage, punctuation, and spelling. Proofreading your essays will help you demonstrate these skills. In this chapter, you will review **proofreading notation** and then will practice proofreading for errors in the following areas of writing:

- **Grammar:** Sentence Types and Formation
- **Usage:** Parts of Speech and Spelling
- **Mechanics:** Capitalization and Punctuation

(If you or your teacher feels more practice or review of grammar would be beneficial, read the text and complete the exercises in American Book Company's companion resources, *Basics Made Easy: Grammar & Usage Review* book and software.)

PROOFREADING NOTATION

Types of handwriting are not graded on the SAT assessments, but if your paper cannot be read, it will not be graded. So, write neatly and clearly, even for your proofreading corrections. **Proofreading notation** refers to certain ways of making corrections that are standard among writers and editors. Some marks used for proofreading notation are shown below.

EDITING AND PROOFREADING CHART

Symbol	Meaning	Example
sp	spelling error	They're ~~Their~~ back from vacation. (sp)
cap	capitalization error	E W I live in the ~~e~~ast, but my sister lives in the ~~w~~est. (cap)
. ? !	end marks	Where are you going ⁄ (?)
,	comma	Hello, Mr. Ripley (,)
^	add	the Ray went to ^ store.
/	change	children Television teaches ~~kids~~ manners.
frag	fragment	Near Kokomo. (frag)
RO	run-on	He tripped he fell. (RO)
t	tense error	ed Yesterday I walk ^ to school. (t)
s-v	subject-verb agreement	Keisha and I love~~s~~ to shop. (s-v)
mod	misplaced modifier	Quickly, Sam ate the sandwich. (mod)

Notice how the proofreading marks are written neatly and clearly, so that they do not interfere with reading the text. Develop standard abbreviations and notations for editing your writing. Though you do not necessarily need to use these standard markings on the actual SAT essay, they make preparation for the essay a little easier.

GRAMMAR

What are we really referring to when we speak of correct grammar?

Nouns, verbs, objects, indirect objects, articles, prepositions: These simple terms, plus a few others, refer to the building blocks of grammar. **Grammar** merely refers to the way words are put together to form ideas. You've been doing this verbally since you first spoke in complete sentences. For a passing-to-excellent score on the SAT essay, you need to use a variety of complete sentence types from the simple to the compound-complex. You will also need to avoid the errors of sentence fragments, run-on sentences, misplaced modifiers, and others.

SENTENCE TYPES

Sentence types are built from phrases and clauses. **Phrases** and **clauses** are two groups of words that help form the structure of sentences. A phrase is a group of words that acts as a single unit in a sentence, but it lacks either a subject, predicate or both. Phrases can function as nouns, verbs, adjectives, or adverbs. A clause is a group of words which includes a subject and predicate. There are two kinds of clauses: **dependent** and **independent**.

An **independent** clause can stand alone as a sentence.

Example: This sentence is an independent clause.

If another independent clause is linked to it, the two clauses must be joined by a comma and a **coordinating conjunction**. **FANBOYS** is an easy way to remember the common coordinating conjunctions: **f**or, **a**nd, **n**or, **b**ut, **o**r, **y**et, **s**o.

Example: These two clauses are joined, *and* they both have a subject and predicate.

A **dependent** clause relies on the controlling independent clause in a sentence. The independent clause and the dependent clause are linked together by a **relative pronoun** such as *which*, *that*, *whose*, or *those*, or by a subordinating conjunction like *while*, *because*, *since*, or *after*.

Example: Dependent clauses *that appear in the middle of an independent clause* often add clarifying information.

Being able to recognize these different sentence elements is the first step in remembering to use them in your writing. You do not have to memorize the names of sentence types. If you simply practice writing with a variety of sentences, you will boost your SAT essay score. Look at the table on the next page, which lists the types of sentences and gives examples.

Types of Sentences

Simple Sentence: One independent clause — may have a compound subject, a compound predicate, or both may be compound.

subject predicate

Example 1: The *human genome research* is *finished.*

subject subject

Example 2: Many *scientists* and the *public* expected different results.

predicate predicate

Example 3: Researchers *announced* and *explained* results

Compound Sentence: Two or more independent clauses — may be joined by a semi-colon, or by a comma with a coordinating conjunction

1st independent clause 2nd independent clause

Example 1: *The results recorded over 30,000 human genes*, **but scientists had thought there would be 100,000.**

1st independent clause 2nd independent clause

Example 2: *Researchers explained the difference in the amounts*; **each gene sends several messages for inherited traits.**

Complex Sentence: One independent clause and one or more dependent clause(s)

dependent clause independent clause

Example 1: *In the words of natural historian Stephen Jay Gould*, **this is a case of less being truly more.**

independent clause dependent clause

Example 2: *Many people think* that **only complex systems can define humans.**

1st dependent clause

Example 3: Those *who trust the value of simplicity* will appreciate the elegance of

2nd dependent clause

the human genome, since **few things in life are as clear and refined.**

Compound-complex Sentence: Two or more independent clauses and one or more dependent clause(s)

dependent clause 1st independent clause

Example 4: *In a rare display of symbolism*, **the human genome research**

2nd independent clause

announcement was given on February 12, 2001; <u>the date is the anniversary of Charles Darwin's birth.</u>

When you proofread your practice essays, note how many types of sentences you use. Do you tend to repeat one type of sentence more than others without a break? If you typically write a string of simple sentences, you can combine two of them by using a semi-colon between them or by using a comma with a conjunction. If you tend to write more compound sentences, use a period at the end of the first independent clause and start the next with a capital — creating two simple sentences.

TIP

Self-awareness in the process of writing will help you to "write it right" the first time.

More Sentence Variety

Using a variety of sentences also includes using sentences with different purposes — write more than just the plain **declarative sentences** (ending with periods). You will want to sprinkle a few **interrogatory sentences** (questions) ending with question marks (?). You may use an **exclamatory sentence**, ending with an exclamation point (!). These would most likely be used in an opinion essay based on personal experience. End punctuation can add to the organization and variety of your writing.

Examples: [**declarative**] The different ways to end sentences are periods, question marks and exclamation points. [**interrogative**] Did you hear what one famous writer said about using the exclamation point? [**exclamatory**] The writer said that using exclamation points in your writing is like laughing at your own jokes!

Sentence Formation

Sentence formation is one of the key writing elements that the SAT essay section will evaluate. To demonstrate skill in this area, you must use clear, complete sentences by correcting any sentence fragments and run-ons, correctly punctuating phrases and clauses, and avoiding misplaced and dangling modifiers.

Sentence Fragments and Run-On Sentences

Punctuation errors can result in sentence fragments and run-ons. A **sentence fragment** is a phrase that is punctuated like a sentence, but lacks a subject or verb. To correct these, simply add the missing element or attach the phrase to the independent clause with a semi-colon or a comma.

Example: The dream Thoreau had of life lived simply may never be realized. *At least not in the American culture.*

The words in italics make up a phrase which is a fragment. To correct the fragment, the period could be changed to a comma and the *A* could be changed to the lower case; these changes would attach the phrase to the sentence.

Correct: The dream Thoreau had of life lived simply may never be realized, *at least not in the American culture.*

A **run-on** occurs when two independent clauses are joined with no punctuation or connecting word between them. The combining of independent clauses requires a semi-colon or a comma with its coordinating conjunction. (Remember the list of FANBOYS.)

Example: I wanted to go to the new aquarium and see the exhibits I got sick the day before we were supposed to leave.

Correct: I wanted to go to the new aquarium and see the exhibits, *but* I got sick the day before we were supposed to leave.

Misplaced and Dangling Modifiers

A modifier is a word, phrase or clause that helps clarify the meaning of another word by describing it in more detail. However, if a modifier is positioned incorrectly in a sentence, it may confuse or frustrate the reader.

A **misplaced modifier** is positioned in the sentence too far from what it is modifying. This confuses the meaning, as in the following example.

Example: She could see the crow *easily* flying to its nest.

In this example, it seems from its position in the sentence that the adverb "swiftly" is modifying the verb "could see," but that is not logical. The writer most likely intended to describe how the crow was "flying." To correct this problem, place the modifying clause closer to the word that it describes.

Correct: She could *easily* see the crow flying to its nest.

Limiting modifiers must be treated a little differently. These are words like *almost*, *barely*, *even*, *hardly*, *just*, *merely*, *nearly*, *only*, and *simply*. Usually these words need to be positioned immediately before the words they modify or the sentence meaning will be ambiguous. See the two examples below. The first has an ambiguous meaning, but the second is logical.

Example: The scientists *almost* raised seven million dollars for genetic research.

Correct: The scientists raised *almost* seven million dollars for genetic research.

Dangling modifiers are words that modify an implied or suggested idea in the sentence—but the idea is not actually part of the sentence. They usually appear at the beginnings or ends of sentences. See the example below.

Example: *Living large*, disenchantment with life is often just around the corner.

Does this sentence make sense to you? Who is living large (extravagantly)? Not disenchantment. Obviously, some people may live large. "Living large" is a dangling modifier because its position in the sentence makes it look like it is describing the subject, "disenchantment." Correcting this sentence would mean adding a subject that the modifier could describe or changing the modifier to a phrase. See the corrections.

Correct: Living large, *you may find* disenchantment with life just around the corner.

Correct: *When people live large,* disenchantment is often just around the corner.

Your goal when you are writing is to be clear and logical. Using modifiers incorrectly will confuse your readers. Consider how to make your writing easily understood while using modifiers that add detail and color to your writing. Be aware of the position of modifiers when proofreading.

Practice 1: Grammar

A. Read the following writing prompt on an aspect of human nature and the assignment for an essay. Then read the essay, first for content. Then, scan the essay quickly for errors in grammar. This is half the length of a typical SAT essay, so you will want to finish your search for errors in half the usual time. So spend about two minutes scanning the essay. Make proofreading notations for changes and reword when needed.

Writing Prompt

The natural historian, Stephen Jay Gould, uses the phrase "less is more" when describing the workings of human DNA. There are fewer genes needed for humans than originally thought. The explanation is that each gene is responsible for several types of physical traits. Gould notes that humans tend to not think in terms of less is more — though the natural world tends to seek simple, elegant systems.

Assignment: What is your opinion on the validity or truth that "less is more?" Plan and write an essay in which you develop your point of view (opinion) on this issue. Support your opinion with reasons and evidence brought from your own experience, your studies, or from your observations.

Essay

Less is More Than You Think

We need to turn down the "buy more" roar from advertisers. We need to turn this down from our communities, too. The process of living with less will not be painless. But, it will be simple. As simple as the urging from Henry David Thoreau, who wrote, "Simplify. Simplify."

The process of living with less will bring people more rewards than is immediately apparent. It will bring peace of mind. When bills must be paid, people will have fewer bills. It will bring respect for individuals at their own worth, instead of the false respect for what they own. It will bring back a life based on strong values like integrity, hard work, and community spirit. This instead of a life based on the value of possessions.

To paraphrase President John Kennedy, ask not what your money will buy for you, ask what you can do to buy your money the time to grow. And how it can do genuine good. Continually buying the latest gadgets can get boring. Whether they are tiny but better music players, or faster, flashier vehicles, people set themselves up for disappointment and a constant yearning for the next new thing. Their money disappears down the insatiable hole of conspicuous consumption. Freedom from want cannot be made a law; it is a freedom people can only give to themselves when they stop wanting new things. A life lived free from want, focused on simple needs, is a priceless reward.

B. Write a paragraph describing any pattern of errors found in this essay, and how you corrected them. In your paragraph, use the suggestions for appropriate grammar learned in this section.

USAGE

Usage seems like such a general word. What is meant by usage in writing?

Writing **usage** refers to how words are chosen and used together to form clear ideas. How do you normally use sentence building blocks? Are your subjects and verbs agreeing in number and tense? Are you using the correct forms of adjectives, including the superlatives? When you are writing, and later proofreading, you will want to make sure you have followed the rules for standardized American English. Look for any pattern of errors in the usage of nouns, articles, pronouns, adjectives, adverbs, negative words, verbs, and subject-verb agreement. Usage can also refer to spelling and formal or informal language. When you are writing the SAT essay, you will want to use mostly formal language and sentence construction.

(If you or your teacher feels more practice or review of usage would be beneficial, read the text and complete the exercises in American Book Company's companion resources, *Basics Made Easy: Grammar & Usage Review* book and software.)

NOUNS

Nouns are words which name people, places, things, ideas, and concepts. Common nouns name general examples of these. Proper nouns name specific people, places, things, ideas, and concepts, and are capitalized. Proper nouns are capitalized and common nouns are not. There is a special group of nouns called collective nouns. Collective nouns name single units made up of many members. Two examples are a school of fish and a committee of delegates.

Nouns may be possessive, showing ownership or a relationship. Nouns may also be singular or plural. See the following table for forms of plural nouns:

Singular	Plural	Singular	Plural	Singular	Plural
frame	frames	octopus	octopuses or octopi	tax	taxes
tornado	tornadoes	popcorn	popcorn	wish	wishes
crop	crops	ferry	ferries	story	stories
trench	trenches	flesh	flesh	alumnus	alumni
calf	calves	play	plays	wife	wives
potato	potatoes	elephant	elephants	shelf	shelves
taste	tastes	deer	deer	cactus	cacti

ARTICLES

In English, **articles** like *the* or *a* are closely associated with nouns. These small words often give the reader essential information about the noun they accompany. There are three forms of articles:

- definite the
- indefinite a / an
- zero no article

The first form, the definite article, is *the*. It can be used with any type of noun. *The* marks a thing that is known to readers either by general knowledge, the context of the rest of the writing, or by the information in the noun phrase.

Example: The research into *the* number of human genes is done.

There are three instances where *the* is always needed:

- Before the word same (the **same** idea of "less is more")
- Generally before a written (ordinal) number (the **first** step to take)
- Before a superlative statement (the **best** scientific research)

The indefinite article, *a* / *an*, does not identify a certain thing. The writer may know of the particular noun item but does not expect the reader to know it. The indefinite *a* / *an* can only be used with singular nouns. The article **a** is used before a word that begins with a consonant letter or sound. The article **an** is used before words that begin with a vowel letter or sound.

Example: I read **a** science magazine. He worked on **a** new invention.

Example: We had **an** idea. We walked **an h**our to get there.

The third form, the **zero article**, means no article at all. No articles are used with plural or uncounted nouns. Often, vague generalizations are made with no article.

Example: We will study astronomy next.

PRONOUNS

Pronouns take the place of nouns. A pronoun must agree in number and gender with the noun it replaces. Some examples of pronouns are *I*, *you*, *she*, *he*, *it*, *we*, *they*, *us*, *their*, *who*, *that*, *them*, *someone*, *whose*, *none*, and *nobody*. Some of these pronouns may act as adjectives when they are followed by a noun, for example *that*, *those*, or *these*. Also, some pronouns may begin a question, for example *what*, *who*, or *whose*.

Example 1: *I* think *we* could change school policy about science research if *we* keep *our* suggestions about *it* simple.

Example 2: When we make *these* suggestions, we must frame *them* respectfully.

Example 3: *What* will be our backup plan if the answer is no to new research?

Adjectives

Adjectives are words which modify, or describe, nouns and pronouns. They may be words which describe how something looks: color, size, weight, shape, etc. Adjectives can also describe texture, quality, and emotional elements. Adjectives answer the questions *Which? How many?* or *What kind?* In contrast to many other languages, English almost always places adjectives before the word or words that they modify. One exception is seen in sentences which have *state of being* verbs; for example, "This exam is *easy.*" The verb *is* signals state of being, and the word *easy* describes the test as an adjective. Pronouns and articles can also function as adjectives when followed by a noun.

Example 1: Our *one brilliant* backup plan is *simple* but *strategic.*

Example 2: We will wave *a white* flag of surrender and wait to fight *our* battle *another* day.

Adverbs

Adverbs are used to modify many different kinds of words. Adverbs can modify verbs, adjectives, or other adverbs. Frequently, adverbs end in -ly, but not always. All adverbs answer one of these questions: *Where? When? In what manner?* or *To what extent?* One common adverb is the word *not.*

Example 1: *Frankly,* I think that idea is *simply not* tenable.

[*Frankly* modifies rest of the sentence, and *simply* and *not* modify tenable]

Example 2: Waving a white flag has a *marginally* honorable history, yes, but in this case it *truly* indicates strong scientific beliefs.

[*Marginally* modifies honorable, and *truly* modifies indicates]

Adjectives and adverbs are also used to compare or weigh differences. The comparative form of adjectives and adverbs (*-er*) is used to compare two things. The superlative form of adjectives and adverbs (*-est*) is used to compare three or more things.

NOTE: For words with one syllable, use the *-er* and *-est* ending. For words with two or more syllables, place *more, most, less,* or *least* in front of the comparing adjective or adverb. If the comparison is negative, use the words *worse* (two things) or *worst* (three or more things).

Example 1: Did you say you have a *bigger* flag than this one?

Example 2: We could have a contest to find the *most impressive* flag in the school.

Negative Words

Two **negative words** cannot be used to express one negative idea. When they are, it is called a double negative. Unfortunately, it is one of the most common errors in English. Negative words include *nothing, not, nearly, never, hardly, neither,* and *no one.*

Example: I *can't hardly* believe you want to wave a real white flag.

Correct: I *can hardly* believe you want to wave a real white flag.

Verbs

A verb is a word or group of words which make up a part of *every* complete sentence. A verb can describe action which the subject takes or receives, or can link the subject to another word which describes it. Verbs must agree with the subject in a sentence in number and person, and verbs change tense to indicate the time of action.

Consider how you use verbs in sentences and essays. Generally speaking, a verb tense should not change within an essay without a logical reason, but verbs do shift in number with the subject of the sentence.

Subject-Verb Agreement

Subject-verb agreement means that both the subject and the verb of a sentence or clause must be of the same number and person. For example, a singular subject must be paired with a singular verb, and a noun in the first person must be paired with a verb in the first person. Consider how you use verbs to agree with subjects.

Example 1: A gene sends messages to form individual human traits.

Example 2: Genes send these messages through DNA.

Subject-Verb Agreement with Collective Nouns

Collective nouns name single units made of multiple members. Collective nouns have special rules regarding agreement with verbs. If the unit is truly acting as one, the singular verb is used reflecting the singular subject. However, if the unit's members act individually then the verb reflects the plural nature of the subject.

Example 1. A swarm of bees lives in this hive.

Example 2: The court had dissenting opinions on how to legislate natural areas.

Proofreading for collective noun errors concerns the verb form used with them. Think about the logic of using the singular and plural form with the action that is occurring. Is it a group action or individual action?

Spelling

Spelling is the process of arranging letters to form words. This may seem simple, but spelling English words can be difficult. The English language has a history of taking words from other languages and trying to make this spelling fit the rules of standardized American English. These rules are rather inconsistent, making spelling twice as difficult. This chapter will provide you with hints and practice in finding homonyms and incorrect spellings while you proofread. Also, there are Web sites recommended at the end of this chapter which have lists of commonly confused homonyms and commonly misspelled words. (SP is an editing abbreviation for misspelled.)

Examples: recieved(sp)-received; enviroment(sp)-environment; Tennesee(sp)-Tennessee; abreviation(sp)-abbreviation, etc.

Homonyms

Homonyms are words that sound the same, even though they have different spellings and meanings. The best way to proofread for errors in the use of homonyms is to recognize the homonyms you tend to misuse and look for those first. You may also want to find a list of the most commonly misused homonyms. Study the list so you can recognize common errors. (See end of chapter.)

Examples: plane/plain; rain/reign; blew/blue; pear/pare; cell/sell; council/counsel, and so on.

Incorrect Spellings

Incorrect spellings of words can make your writing sloppy or confusing. Because so many words in English have irregular spellings, it is important to memorize commonly misspelled words. It is also helpful to follow a plan when proofreading for spelling errors.

First, consider the spelling errors that are typical for you, and look for those types of errors. Second, think about the basic structure of forming words and correct any words that do not follow the structure. Last, use your sight memory — the memory which tells you when something just does not look right — and correct the word so it looks right. Using this plan, your proofreading for spelling should be successful. When practicing for the SAT essay, you may want to use a notebook for a spelling journal. Make a list of words that you frequently misspell. Write them ten times each for practice. (Also see end of chapter for sites with misspelled word lists.)

Practice 2: Usage

A. This essay is written from the same writing prompt and assignment as Practice 1. Read the following essay, first for content. Then scan the essay for errors in usage. This is half the length of a typical SAT essay, so you will want to finish your search in half the time. Spend about two minutes scanning the essay and making proofreading notations for changes.

Less Is More Than What?

The statement "less is more" still leaves the possibility of ownership, of health, of life. So what could less be more than, literrally? There is only one possibility as to what less is more than; less is more than zero. Consider that for an moment. Less of something implies that there is an amount that you can measure. Maybe it cannot be measured exactly; the term "less" gives no clues by itself of its quantity. However, the same cannot be said of the number zero. Zero means exactly nada, zilch, none, nothing. And that scares the fool out of many people around the world.

Why would people shy away from the number zero? Zero is a fairly recent invention in the world of mathematics. It was created in either India or Arabia by mathamaticians in about the second or seventh century (the history is murky). Before the invention of zero, all calculations began with the number one. If you had one apple and ate them, how many apples would you have left? There was no word for this. And you can see why it could be a frightening idea. If you have no apples, you could starve. You could die from having nothing. A common symptom of this fear is the practice of using the letter "O" to express verbally the number zero.

So the next time you here that less is more, hear it with a feeling of gratitude. It means that there is more than nothing — there is more than zero in your life. Ultimate loss and extreme deprivation is not lurking outside your door, and the abyss of eternity is far away. Life can be rich and full and glorious, even, and maybe even especially, when there is less.

B. Write a paragraph describing any pattern of errors found in this essay, and how you corrected them. In your paragraph, use the suggestions for appropriate usage learned in this section.

MECHANICS

We use the word **mechanics** to describe the smallest, most common, yet vital points in writing: **capitalization** and **punctuation**. No matter what other skills you possess for writing a passing-to-excellent SAT essay, you will be using these two aspects of writing.

CAPITALIZATION

Capitalization involves the practice of using a mixture of capital letters ("A") and lower case letters ("a"). In modern English, there are rules for capitalizing certain words in order to emphasize their importance. One example is the first word of a sentence, like the word "**One**," which began this sentence. Another example of words that are capitalized is proper nouns, like "**S**an **M**ateo, **C**alifornia." There are many other examples of times when a word should be capitalized, such as the words in titles. Think for a moment about the examples that you know.

If you are uncertain about capitalization rules, see the rules and practices in American Book Company's companion resources, *Basics Made Easy: Grammar & Usage Review* book and software. You may also want to practice using these materials.

PUNCTUATION

Punctuation marks add clarity, emphasis, and conviction to your essay. Granted, they can also be confusing, self-contradictory, and hard to understand. Fortunately, the SAT essay test falls somewhere between these two extremes. To score well, you do not *have* to have a scholar's approach to punctuation, but you do need a competent working knowledge. Writing well as a rule requires a firm grasp anyway, so all practice in this area you make for the SAT will automatically benefit other areas of your life.

COMMAS

The action of writing an essay has a certain flow and thought process in drafting and even proofing. This flow can create an engaging paper, but can also lead to omissions of certain punctuation. Commas are often forgotten in the flow of writing. Proofreading for any missing commas is important for the clarity of your paper.

Commas can signal a contrast, set off extra information, signal direct address, or separate items in lists. There are other uses for commas as well. Consider what you know about using commas.

> **Example 1:** Science is absolute, but also changeable.
>
> **Example 2:** That is one of the paradoxes in life, meaning that it is a mystery.
>
> **Example 3:** What do you, dear reader, think of this?
>
> **Example 4:** Never can science replace the treasures of life: mystery, poetry, loving, dreaming, imagining, and reaching out to the unknown.

Colons, Semi-Colons, and Apostrophes

A **colon** signals a bit of information that the sentence needs. It most often sets off a list, a quotation, an appositive (renaming), an explanation or an example. Colons are also used in number phrases like time notations or Biblical references.

> **Example 1:** The newest additions to dictionaries originated in science and technology: blog, genome, bunny suit, data glove, phishing, and zipperhead.
>
> **Example 2:** This scientist had an enthusiastic entreaty for audiences: "Remember, it's a gift to be simple and to freely rejoice in the span of stars."
>
> **Example 3:** The span of stars have many names: the most easily understood name is galaxy.
>
> **Example 4:** The best time to view the span of stars in most areas of the US begins at about 9:30 pm and ends about 4:30 am.

Two major rules about the colon are:

- never place it right after a verb (between the verb and its object) but if adding the phrase *the following* or *below*—the colon may be used, and
- never use it to separate two independent clauses with a coordinating conjunction between them—this construction calls for a comma.

> **Example 1:** The top reason to follow the less/more equation is: genetic research.
>
> **Correction:** The top reason to follow the less/more equation: genetic research.
>
> **Example 2:** Genetic research promises to cure disease: but it has great potential for aberrations in this area.
>
> **Correction:** Genetic research promises to cure disease, but it has great potential for aberrations in this area.

Semi-colons may be used to separate two independent clauses which are closely related to one idea. (For more emphasis, you may also use a colon in this case, especially to emphasize the second clause.) Another common use of the semi-colon is to separate items in a list when the item names contain commas.

> **Example 1:** Pioneers in genetic research proceed carefully; they wish to benefit people.
>
> **Example 2:** Our clubs following genetic research are quite divergent in interests, such as the Art Council Club, whose goal is to render scientific discoveries in a visual medium; the Environmental Science Club, whose purpose is to record genetic changes in the wildlife; the Debate Team Club, which is always looking for fresh topics to debate; and the Agricultural Club (formerly

Farmers of America), which is monitoring the effects of genetic engineering on crops, bees, butterflies, and people.

Apostrophes do not separate anything; they signal either possession or missing letters in contractions.

Example 1: Our club's bylaws mention genetic research.

Example 2: You'll see it there just before the entries on rock'n' roll and o'clock.

Quotation Marks

Quotation marks are frame words that belong to someone besides the author. When used in fiction, quotation marks help to keep the voices of different characters from becoming confused. They also frame titles of short works. There are two types of quotation marks:

- double quotation marks (“ ”) are used to signal direct writing prompts or some titles
- single quotation marks (‘ ’) are used to signal writing prompts within writing prompts

Example 1: The president of the Procrastinator's Club said, “We will look into how we feel about genetic research after our annual non-meeting.”

Example 2: The title of the Procrastinator's handbook declares “Less is More.”

Example 3: One member made this suggestion: “Let's change the name of our handbook to ‘Much to Do about Nothing’ since it is a classic and so appropriate.”

Example 4: I seconded the motion saying, “We have too long settled for less, and now, as Thoreau said, ‘Simplify and live with nothing,’ so we can truly put off everything!”

Practice 3: Mechanics

A. This essay is another response to the writing prompt and essay in Practice 1. Read first for content, then scan quickly for errors in mechanics. This is half the length of a typical SAT essay, so you will want to finish your search for errors in half the usual time. Spend about two minutes scanning the essay and making proofreading notations for changes.

One Person's Experience with Less

Less is more . . . Benjamin Franklin would have liked this three-word philosophy- -it sounds like his ‘A penny saved is a penny earned.’ In his day, I bet a penny would have bought at least two Videos, if they had had them, that is. Now it is just a fairy tale, too. Who can get by on saving pennies or by having less instead of more?

I tried it for a while the “less thing.” I ate only raw almonds, tofu jelly, and drank water with no ice. I was experiencing the euphoria of being “better than anyone” at living with less. I bought only used CDs, no fancy player/storage gizmo for me. I got clothes at yard sales and brushed my teeth with baking soda. But it was when I used lemon juice and vinegar as underarm deodorant that I started losing friends for real. They put up with party's featuring only local educational TV Stations for entertainment and day-old doughnuts for food — but personal hygiene on the cheap; that crossed the line

"Less" friends is not more: never! So, I started buying designer soaps and teeth whiteners, too. I installed satellite TV and got the latest computerized miniaturized CD player. Now my clothes come from the uptown mall and my food is prepared at the best fast food restaurants: you know the one's using canola oil for frying. Raw almonds are still my favorite food though — only I eat more of them now.

B. Write a paragraph describing any pattern of errors found in this essay, and how you corrected them. In your paragraph, use the suggestions for appropriate mechanics learned in this section.

Student Resources: Web Sites and Books

Spelling

Commonly Misspelled Words List

http://www.library.cornell.edu/tsmanual/TSSU/com[illegible]s1.html

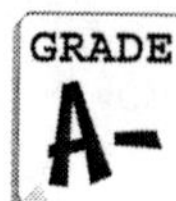

This site is part of the Cornell University Library site. Plain but succinct and thorough — the alphabetical listings display a misspelled word, the correct spelling, the date the word was added to this list, and the number of occurrences. There is a page describing the procedure behind the list-making, but this information is not for the casual reader unless statistics are a favorite topic. The site is low on entertainment and artistic presentation, but high on solid information.

Commonly Misspelled Words

http://grammar.ccu.commnet.edu/grammar

Part of *Guide to Grammar and Writing* site. It is an excellent starting place for anyone who needs to practice from the sentence level to a full research paper. There are quizzes, spelling rules, and a list of commonly misspelled words (taken, the site says, from *Student's* (sic) *Book of College English*).

Usage

Common Errors in English Usage

http://www.wsu.edu/~brians/errors/index.html

Great amount of commonly confused homonyms — arrayed in blue, in alphabetical sequence, separated by asterisks—there are also terms like hoi polloi and quantum leap whose meanings have been confused with overuse. The author of this site, a professor Paul Brians, has taken pains with extras, such as links to literary sites. He has published a book of the same name as this site, for those who prefer hard copy text.

The UVic Writer's Guide: Levels of Use

http://web.uvic.ca/wguide/Pages/SentLevs[illegible]Usage.html

GRADE B

The page presents a discussion of the levels of language usage: formal, informal, and popular. There are examples and guidelines for choosing the best language usage suited to the writing task. Good information but narrow in scope.

Mechanics

The Nuts and Bolts of College Writing

http://nutsandbolts.washcoll.edu/mechanics.html

This is not just for college students! It is a colorful site with a toolbox theme and plenty of information on all aspects of writing. There is a "Top Ten Mistakes List" and many other topics listed. There are also writing prompts inserted into the instructional text.

Books

Jane Straus. The Blue Book of Grammar and Punctuation. Mill Valley: Jane Strauss, 2004.

Another excellent turorial on grammar and punctuation, this book is written in a style at once friendly and perfectionist. Includes exercises, and tests, and guide sheets.

Lynne Truss. Eats Shoots, & Leaves: The Zero Tolerance Approach to Punctuation. New York: Gotham, 2004.

This perennial bestseller takes a light, witty touch in explaining the importance of grammar in everyday life and gives a thorough explanation of the "workhorses" of punctuation, especially pronouns.

Published 2003 by Gotham Books — London and New York

Chapter 5 Review

A. Look back to the essay you wrote for the chapter review in **Chapter 4**. Proofread this essay based on the skills that you have practiced in this chapter.

You may want to use the checklist below to help you. When you finish, give the essay with its changes to your teacher or share it with a classmate.

- ❑ **I made my corrections neatly and clearly.**
- ❑ **I looked for a variety of sentence types.**
- ❑ **I looked for errors in sentence formation, including end punctuation, fragments, run-ons, and misplaced modifiers.**
- ❑ **I checked for errors in capitalization.**
- ❑ **I corrected errors in internal punctuation—including commas, colons, semi-colons, apostrophes, and quotation marks.**
- ❑ **I corrected any errors in grammar and usage—including nouns, pronouns, adjectives, adverbs, negative words, verbs, and subject-verb agreement.**
- ❑ **I made sure all words are spelled correctly.**

B. Now that you have practiced proofreading for errors, you will practice writing your essay right the first time. Your awareness for correct grammar, usage, and mechanics has been finely tuned by this chapter. Read the following writing prompts and assignments. Choose one and write an opinion essay in 25 minutes, following the process of planning and writing with an eye to keeping one opinion and voice. You will be writing with a variety of sentences and correct usage and mechanics. If you have time remaining from the 25 minutes, do a quick proofread of your essay.

Writing prompt

"We live in a time of transition . . . During the period we may be tempted to abandon some of the time-honored principles and commitments which have been proven during the difficult times of past generations. We must never yield to this temptation. Our American values are not luxuries, but necessities — not the salt in our bread, but the bread itself."

President Jimmy Carter

Assignment: What is your opinion on the way freedoms should be managed, if at all? Plan and write an essay in which you develop your point of view on the issue. Support your opinion with reasons and evidence brought from your own experience, your studies, or from your observations.

Writing Prompt

The idea of freedom is one that different cultures and different people interpret in different ways. Recently the Russian government said it has its own type of democracy; different perhaps from that of the U.S., but a democracy all the same. And from his position as India's spiritual leader, Mahatma Ghandi said, "Freedom is not worth having if it does not include the freedom to make mistakes."

Assignment: What is your opinion on how the ideal of freedom should be interpreted? Plan and write an essay in which you develop your point of view (opinion) on the issue. Support your opinion with reasons and evidence brought from your own experience, your studies, or from your observations.

Ask a teacher or peer to give you feedback on your essay, verbally or on a separate sheet of paper. Then put the essay in your portfolio. You will use it in the next chapter.

Chapter 6
Improving Sentences, the SAT Way

Introducing

the Interaction-Driven, New and "You-Improved" SAT Sentences!

We are employing this shameless commercial setup to get you ready, able, and more than willing to practice improving sentences for the SAT. The testing format is one you will most likely appreciate. You will not be required to know the names of the embedded errors or the improvements—you simply need to recognize any errors and determine the best way to correct them.

TIPS

1. **Remember** that several of the test sentences will be "error-less." When a test sentence seems correct as it appears, then Choice A, the exact replica of the original sentence, is the choice you will want to make.
2. **Keep in mind** that the correct responses will rarely, if ever, include being or –ing verbs.
3. **Choose** the response that is concise, clear, and true to the original meaning of the testing sentence.
4. **Eliminate** any obvious incorrect responses and focus on choosing the most clearly written choice.
5. **Some texts** may advise you that when in doubt you should choose the shortest choice (least wordy), but beware: the test creators know of this maneuver and will have adjusted many choices accordingly.

Within the improving sentences items, the embedded errors, when present, will be in one of the following areas:

Grammar	This refers to syntax or the order of forms of speech used in English language sentences. The most common order, for example, is *subject-verb-object*. some of the subtopics for grammar are as follows: • passive voice • pronoun-antecedent agreement
Punctuation	This is the area comprising the tools of language, marking or signaling textual elements in sentences. Some of the subtopics for punctuation include: • end-punctuation • commas • semi-colons • colons
Sentence Construction	This area embraces the basic construction of sentences, enabling writers to logically communicate ideas. Some of the subtopics for sentence construction are: • conjunctions • fragments • parallelism • run-ons • misplaced modifiers
Word Choice	This concerns effectively choosing words for their concise and precise meanings, also known as vocabulary and diction. Some of the subtopics for word choice are: • flawed word choices • wordiness • idioms (prepositions)

The subtopics in the preceding chart comprise most of the specific errors you are expected to recognize and correct through multiple-choice options. This chapter will briefly review each of the specific errors.

If you would like more information or practice, see the proofreading chapter of this text or use the listing of Web sites and texts at the end of this chapter as a starting point for improving writing at the sentence level.

GRAMMAR

When the order of words in a sentence produces awkward or unorganized meaning, the order needs correcting.

Passive Voice

Grammar in the passive voice is "switched" — instead of subject-verb-object, it is object-verb-subject. This produces a slower thought process, and reads awkwardly. When the subject and verb are paired together, the action is much more direct and dynamic.

Example: The newest Driver's Ed class *will be taken* by our school's juniors first.

The Driver's Ed class is not performing the verb — it will not be taking something. The junior class is the subject. Clues to this passive voice construction include the use of the word "by" after the verb, and the use of past participle verbs (in this case "taken") with the auxiliary verbs to be.

Correction: Our school's juniors *will take* the newest Driver's Ed class.

Pronoun-antecedent Agreement

Here's a trick for help with pronoun-antecedent agreement:

Pronoun-antecedent agreement can be complicated, or *it* may be complicated.

In the rule above, "it" is a pronoun that replaces the lengthy **antecedent** phrase "Pronoun-antecedent agreement." The pronoun is singular and gender-neutral, like the noun it replaces, so they are said to agree. But consider these more complicated grammar constructions with pronoun-antecedent agreements.

Pronouns agreeing with compound antecedents, which happens when two or more nouns are joined by the conjunction *and*. In this instance, the pronoun must be plural.

Example. Senators *and* the president alike must agree on *their* agenda for the diplomatic trip.

Because two parties — in this case, the president and the senators — must agree on something, the pronoun is plural. (They already agree with themselves.) But when the compound antecedent comes after *each* or *every* the pronoun becomes singular.

Example: *Each* rock and tree has *its* charm and story to tell.

The pronoun is the singular *its* (instead of the plural *their*) because, while the rocks and trees have something in common, the use of each implies the individual stories would be told separately.

Having pronouns agree with collective-noun antecedents has two possibilities for construction. **1**) When a collective noun refers to *individual* members of a unit, the pronoun will be <u>plural</u>. **2**) When a collective noun refers *to the complete unit*, the pronoun will be <u>singular</u>.

Example: The *herd* of bison scattered towards *their* favorite places at the river.

Example: The *herd* of bison thundered past us in tight formation, protecting *its* young.

Having pronouns agree with indefinite-pronoun antecedents mostly depends on the logic of the text. Some indefinite pronouns like "one" will always take the singular pronoun, while some indefinite pronouns like "several" always takes the plural pronoun. Then others, like "some," depend on the context.

Example: *One* of the horses threw *its* shoe during the race.

Example: *Several* of the children left for *their* field trip carrying cameras.

Example: *Some* of the lawyers offered *their* free time to help with the debate team.

Example: *Some* of the music needed *its* tempo tweaked.

Practice 1: Grammar

The sentences in this practice allow you to assess the correctness and effectiveness of expression. In choosing responses, use the expectations set by standard written English.

In the sentences below, part of the sentence or the whole sentence is underlined. Beneath these sentences you will find four ways of re-phrasing the underlined part. Choose the response that best expresses the meaning of the original sentence. Choose A if you think the original is correct. Choose one of the others if it is an improvement. Your choice should create the most effective sentence — clear and precise, without awkwardness or ambiguity.

1. After lunch, <u>the prize for the best barbecue recipe will be awarded by the judge</u>.

   A. leave as is
   B. the prize signifying the best barbecue recipe will be awarded by the judge
   C. awarded the prize for the best barbecue recipe by the judge
   D. the judge will award the prize for the best barbecue recipe
   E. the award for the prize barbecue recipe took place by the judge

2. Our chorus <u>ensemble takes their next working road trip to Boston</u>.

   A. leave as is
   B. Boston the ensemble will be taking the next working road trip
   C. by Boston takes the ensemble on its next working road trip
   D. ensemble takes their next road trip working at Boston
   E. ensemble takes its next working road trip to Boston

3. Citizens know Chicago as the windy city originally because <u>of their reputation of having local councilmen yelling loud, windy boasts</u> about the city's glories.

   A. leave as is
   B. of their reputation of having local councilmen who yelled loud, windy boasts
   C. of its reputation of local councilmen yelling loud, windy boasts
   D. the reputation of having local councilmen that yelled boasts
   E. of how it has a reputation of local councilmen who yelled loud, windy boasts

View of Chicago

4. Raspberries grow equally well in Atlanta and Seattle most likely because of similar rainfall, <u>and if they are harvested daily by gardeners, a fresh home supply is guaranteed.</u>

   A. leave as is
   B. and if it's harvested daily by gardeners, a fresh home supply are guaranteed
   C. and if then they are harvested at least daily, a fresh supply is guaranteed
   D. and if harvested daily by gardeners, a fresh home supply is guaranteed
   E. and if gardeners harvest them daily, a fresh supply is guaranteed

5. Margaret and Sam have been my two favorite characters on the series *West Wing*, <u>although the roles are not leading ones</u>.

   A. leave as is
   B. although their roles are secondary
   C. although it is not leading roles
   D. but that their roles are not the leading ones
   E. the roles are not leading

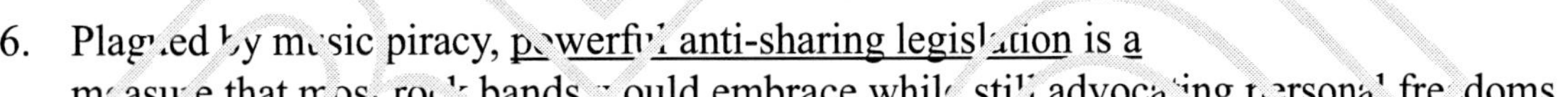

6. Plagued by music piracy, <u>powerful anti-sharing legislation is a measure that most rock bands would embrace while still advocating</u> personal freedoms.

   A. leave as is
   B. anti-sharing legislation that is a measure that most rock bands would embrace while still advocating
   C. most rock bands would embrace powerful anti-sharing legislation while still advocating
   D. powerful anti-sharing legislation are measures that most rock bands would embrace while advocating
   E. rock bands would embrace powerful anti-sharing legislation as a measure, while still advocating

"Gosh-Awful" Grammar Details

Most grammar rules help us to make sense in writing and speaking with each other. Some rules defy this generalization, but are still rules to be observed. Review the list of "Gosh-Awful" grammar details following.

Rule 1. **The "Than" Rule:** When comparing one object to another, be careful if the word *than* is used. Remember, the entire object being compared must be noted.

Incorrect: My new laptop computer is so much better than my old desktop.

Logically, the sentence compares a computer to a desktop. Complete the comparison.

Correct: My new laptop computer is so much better than my old desktop computer.

Rule 2. **The 'Subordination" Clause:** When a subordinating conjunction is used, a dependent clause should follow — which includes a subject and a verb. See example below:

Incorrect: The field trip was canceled because of apparently assigned writing with errors by sloppiness.

The phrase following 'because" does not have a subject and verb.

Correct: The field trip was canceled because the assigned writing had too many errors caused by sloppiness.

Rule 3. **Extended Parallelism:** No matter how convoluted and involved a sentence seems, keep an eye on the structures for parallelism. See example below:

Incorrect: The animal hospital in the metro area, staffed and operated with a small crew, took in animals which were lost in woods, had been abandoned, or were simply irritating their owners.

Each verb in the series should be in the same tense.

Correct: The animal hospital in the metro area, staffed and operated with a small crew, took in animals which were lost, abandoned, or unloved.

Rule 4. **Levels of Modifiers:** Modifiers of course must be used near the noun being modified. This can get tricky with pronouns. See an example below:

Incorrect: He was looking to sign a message to Koko, the gorilla, but in studying her movements, she did not behave as though interested in eating at the moment.

As the sentence stands, the gorilla is studying her own behavior as the modifying prepositional phrase comes immediately after the pronoun "she."

Correct: He was looking to sign a message to Koko, the gorilla, but a study of her behavior showed she behaved as though not interested in eating at the moment.

Rule 5. **Idiomatic Prepositions:** This is a wide open category; these are elements which come with use of the English language.

Incorrect: Suffice **for** say, watch **at** prepositions which do not fit **to** the moment **in** time.

Correct: Suffice **to** say, watch **for** prepositions which do not fit **in** the moment **of** time.

Punctuation

Punctuation offers signals showing readers where ideas separate and where they blend together. Punctuation may signal contrasting elements or complimentary elements.

End-Punctuation

End punctuation signals when a sentence is complete. It also signals the type of sentence: statement, with period; question, with question mark; or exclamation with exclamation point.

Example: When a tree falls in the woods, it may land in the creek with a splash.

Example: If a tree falls in the woods onto a moss bed, does it make a noise?

Example: When that tree fell in the woods onto my car, it made a huge noise!

Commas

The use of commas is varied and valuable. Some comma functions are as follows: signaling restatement; separating two independent clauses when paired with a conjunction, or setting off direct address; and separating simple series items.

Plato *Aristotle*

Example: Plato, one of the creators of philosophical thought, developed the image of reality as shadows on a cave wall.

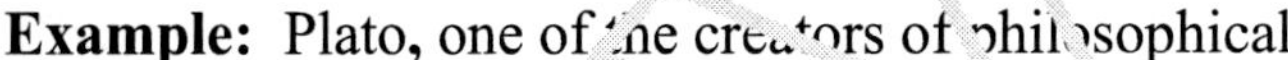

Example: Plato and Aristotle were philosophers in the same age, *and* they motivated each other to achieving ever greater insights.

Example: The philosophy of "the winner takes all" in reality programs seems inane to me, Alexis.

Example: Speaking of Plato's reality as shadows on a wall, its banality is proven by reality programs on television, such as "Survivor," "Beauty and the Geek," "The Apprentice," "The Real Gilligan's Island," "I Want to be a Hilton," and "The Princes of Malibu."

Semi-colons

Semi-colons signal a stronger pause than commas but are used in similar situations. They are used to separate independent clauses (without conjunctions), and they separate complex items in a series.

Example: Ms. Flores said that it was a philosopher who first asked that if a tree falls in the woods does it make a sound if no one is there to hear; this kind of unsolvable question can be used as an ice breaker for people who are getting acquainted.

Example: The membership of our philosophy club may surprise most people as it includes Troy Caballo, a star basketball center; Jason Argon, the high-dive champion; Penelope Weaver, an all-star softball pitcher; and Helen Wu, our top tennis ace.

Colons

A **colon** is a definite break in the flow of text. Some textual uses include signaling new information to be added or attaching a list of items to the sentence.

> **Example:** It is said that History repeats itself**:** at least if it is not remembered and its lessons are not learned.

> **Example:** Another philosopher was the Spanish-born George Santayana; his wrote on many topics such as the following**:** life/death, individuality/society, and knowledge/faith.

Practice 2: Punctuation

The sentences in this practice allow you to assess the correctness and effectiveness of expression. In choosing responses, use the expectations set by standard written English for of punctuation.

In the sentences below, part of the sentence or the whole sentence is underlined. Beneath these sentences you will find four ways of re-phrasing the underlined part. Choose the response that best expresses the meaning of the original sentence. Choose A if you think the original is correct. Choose one of the others if it is an improvement. Your choice should create the most effective sentence — clear and precise, without awkwardness or ambiguity.

1. The formation of Blue Angel jets is astonishing in its precision; and the pilots are to be commended for their bravery and skill.
   - A. leave as is
   - B. The formation of Blue Angel jets is astonishing in its precision; yet
   - C. As astonishing as they are the formation of Blue Angel jets has precision; and
   - D. The formation of Blue Angel jets is astonishing in its precision, and
   - E. The precision of the formation of Blue Angel jets are astonishing, and

2. From where does the enduring courage to face the unfaceable appear and how does a person reach it?
   - A. leave as is
   - B. appears, and how does a person reach it!
   - C. appear and how does a person reach it.
   - D. appear, yet how does a person reach it
   - E. appearing, and how does a person reach it?

3. We will now tackle world problems with the family of powerful tools; topology, geodesics, synergetics, and general systems theory.
   - A. leave as is
   - B. We will now with the family of powerful tools tackle world problems; topology,
   - C. With world problems we will now tackle the family of powerful tools; topology,
   - D. Now we will tackle world problems with powerful tools, topology,
   - E. We will now tackle world problems with the family of powerful tools: topology,

4. To go fishing for dinner is not the same as to go "catching" for <u>dinner, there is always an element of surprise when landing a fish and a philosophical shrug when nothing bites</u>.
   A. leave as is
   B. dinner; there is always an element of surprise when landing a fish and a philosophical shrug when nothing bites.
   C. your dinner, there is always an element of surprise when landing a fish and a philosophical shrug when nothing bites.
   D. dinner; there is always an element of surprise when landing a fish and a philosophical shrug when nothing bites?
   E. there is always an element of surprise for dinner, when landing a fish and a philosophical shrug when nothing bites.

5. <u>The next space shuttle Discovery, is tentatively set for launch</u> on July 24 as NASA officials continue to assess the shuttle's status
   A. leave as is
   B. The next space shuttle; Discovery is tentatively set for launch
   C. The next space shuttle, Discovery, is tentatively set for launch
   D. The next space shuttle, Discovery is tentatively set for launch
   E. The next space shuttle, Discovery, is tentatively set for launch

SENTENCE CONSTRUCTION

The basic construction in sentences must be complete and sturdy. **Conjunctions** should hold the elements together and run-ons must be stopped. **Fragments** must be completed and parallels drawn to keep things equal. **Misplaced modifiers** deserve and should receive logical placement. See the following sections on how to improve these sentence construction elements.

CONJUNCTIONS

Conjunctions are words which join two or more independent clauses in a sentence. The acronym **fanboys** is often used as a *mnemonic* or memory device to remember these conjunctions.

F	**A**	**N**	**B**	**O**	**Y**	**S**
o	n	o	u	r	e	o
r	d	r	t		t	

RUN-ONS

When two independent clauses are put together but lack a conjunction, this is called a **run-on**. The sentence has two ideas in tandem, making it sound rushed.

There are three common methods to correct and improve run-on sentences:

- using a comma and conjunction between the two clauses
- using a semi-colon between the two clauses
- using a period after the first clause and a capital for the second to make the clauses two separate sentences.

See the following example and its three improvements.

Example: The space shuttle may not be ready for launch **in late summer, it may even be delayed till the fall of this year**.

Correction 1: in late summer, *and* it may even be delayed till the fall of this year

Correction 2: in late summer; it may even be delayed till the fall of this year

Correction 3: in late summer. *It* may even be delayed till the fall of this year

FRAGMENTS

View of Beijing, China

This serious sentence error is fairly straightforward and easy to "hear" in text. A sentence fragment is missing either a subject or verb. To correct these fragments, merely add the missing part. A less common example of a sentence fragment is a clause which begins with a subordinating word and is not a question. Add another clause to the subordinate one or combine the subordinate clause to a nearby independent one to create a complete sentence.

Example: Changes in the business culture of emerging, modernizing China.

Correction: Changes in the business culture of emerging, modernizing China allow employees and managers to think outside the historic box.

Example: Making the Chinese economy vibrant and nimble in its reactions to the global market.

Correction: The change in culture is making the Chinese economy vibrant and nimble in its reactions to the global market.

Example: Because China is experiencing change and a revitalization of the economy.

Correction: Because China is experiencing change and a revitalization of the economy, the global market is experiencing change as well.

Parallelism

Think of a log cabin which has logs of differing lengths and angles so that the cabin leans or teeters in uneven lines. Likewise, a sentence will seem disjointed or uneven if the elements within the structure are not parallel. These elements may be items in a series, joined phrases, joined clauses, verb forms, and so on. To make elements in the sentence parallel, simply use the same form for all repeated items in the sentence. In the following examples, note the balance in the sentence elements.

Example: Today's headlines encompass stories of union upheavals, tragic occurrences, and civil reactionaries. (all have a disturbing effect)

Example: Local union leaders are voting *either* to remain with the national organization *or* to disband the local chapter completely. (choice of actions)

Example: News reporters closely scrutinized the unfolding drama *and* many took unprecedented risks near the harrowing scene. (cause and effect)

Example: Scores of citizens took part in the peace march *yet* released pamphlets urging calm in the streets.(series of actions)

Misplaced Modifiers

Using modifiers (words, phrases, or clauses) correctly adds color to writing and expands a reader's understanding of the text. Using the same modifiers in the wrong place causes confusion. Modifiers need to be placed next to the word(s) they modify and should not be used where they may be ambiguous (possibly modifying words both before and after them). To improve a sentence with a misplaced modifier, move the modifier closer to the word(s) to be modified. See the following examples of misplaced modifiers and corrections:

Example: We took photos of the Stanley Steamer motor car with our friends displayed at the famous Stanley Hotel in Colorado.

Correction: We took photos of our friends with the Stanley Steamer motor car displayed at the famous Stanley Hotel in Colorado.

Example: Spouting white steam from side vents, we photographed the Durango train's engine.

Correction: We photographed the Durango train's engine spouting white steam from side vents.

Example: (ambiguous): The silver mine's tour director said when she finished she would take requests for western music.

Correction: The silver mine's tour director said she would take requests for western music when she finished.

Practice 3: Sentence Construction

This practice allows you to assess the correctness and effectiveness of expression. In choosing responses, use the expectations set by standard written English in the area of sentence construction.

In the sentences below, part of the sentence or the whole sentence is underlined. Beneath these sentences you will find four ways of re-phrasing the underlined part. Choose the response that best expresses the meaning of the original sentence. Choose A if you think the original is correct. Choose one of the others if it is an improvement. Your choice should create the most effective sentence — clear and precise, without awkwardness or ambiguity.

1. Nell promised after juggling five pine cones at once she could use three lit torches and a pine branch in her routine.

   A. leave as is
   B. After juggling five pine cones at once, Nell promised she could use
   C. Nell promised after juggling five pine cones, at once, she could use
   D. Nell promised she could use after juggling five pine cones at once,
   E. After she juggled five pine cones, Nell promised, at once, she could use

2. Dennis watched the fireworks display from seventy feet away so he would be safe.

   A. leave as is
   B. From seventy feet away, Dennis watched the fireworks display; so he
   C. So he would be safe Dennis the fireworks display watched from seventy feet away
   D. Dennis watched the fireworks display from seventy feet away, so he
   E. Dennis watched the fireworks display from seventy feet away, he

3. The new car models all have GPS tracking systems, satellite radios, and an ice dispenser serving cubed or crushed ice.

   A. leave as is
   B. each have GPS tracking systems, satellite radios, and an ice dispenser now serving
   C. all have GPS tracking systems, satellite radios, and ice dispensers serving
   D. they all have GPS tracking systems, satellite radios, and an ice dispenser which serves
   E. all having GPS tracking, satellite systems radio and ice dispenser serving

4. Mailing a personal or professional letter through the local traditional blue collection box.

   A. leave as is
   B. Few people have been mailing personal or professional letters through the local, traditional
   C. Mailing a personal or professional letter through the local but traditional
   D. Never be mailing a personal or professional letters through the local, traditional
   E. Resulting from public restraint, mailing a personal or professional letter through the local, traditional

5. The mythological status of <u>Johnny Appleseed is grounded in reality, he planted orchards</u> across the states which stand even today.
   A. leave as is
   B. Johnny Appleseed is grounded in reality, because he planted orchards
   C. Johnny Appleseed is grounded in reality planting orchards
   D. Johnny Appleseed is grounded in reality. Planted orchards
   E. Johnny Appleseed is grounded in reality; he planted orchards

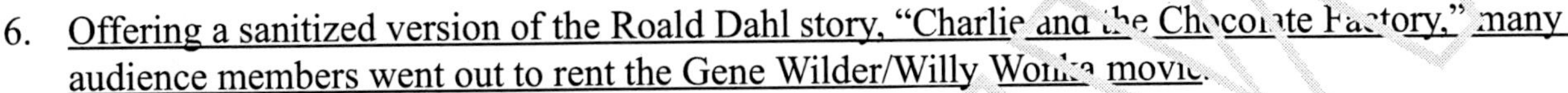

6. <u>Offering a sanitized version of the Roald Dahl story, "Charlie and the Chocolate Factory," many audience members went out to rent the Gene Wilder/Willy Wonka movie.</u>
   A. leave as is
   B. Though really only a sanitized version of the Roald Dahl story "Charlie and the Chocolate Factory," many moviegoers nonetheless turned out for the Gene Wilder movie.
   C. Offering the Roald Dahl story, "Charlie and the Chocolate Factory," many audience members renting a sanitized version of the Gene Wilder/Willy Wonka movie
   D. Many audience members went out to rent the Gene Wilder/Willy Wonka movie that offered a sanitized version of the Roald Dahl story, "Charlie and the Chocolate Factory."
   E. Offering a sanitized version of the Roald Dahl story, "Charlie and the Chocolate Factory," many audience members were renting the Gene Wilder/Willy Wonka movie

Word Choice

Choosing words is partly a matter of **style**, partly a matter of **tone**, and partly a matter of **audience.** These three elements, as well as the topic of a text and the appropriateness of the words themselves, guide the writer on correct word choices. See some common errors and their corrections below:

Flawed Word Choices

If word choice has problems of style, tone, or audience awareness, the text will likely become confusing to the reader. Beware also of errors of homonyms, which are words that sound alike but do not share the same spelling.

Example: Irregardless of good intent, the destruction of historic theaters continues.

Correction: Regardless of good intent, the destruction of historic theaters continues.

Example: The movie paymaster ordered the different denominations on a table for closing night.

Correction: The movie paymaster arranged the different denominations on a table for closing night.

Example: Acting director Mason Broadwell, decided to hang out with his workers in a display of solidarity.

Correction: Acting director Mason Broadwell, decided to remain with his workers in a show of solidarity.

Example: The play's principal actor had sound advise for the whole troupe.

Correction: The play's principle actor had sound advice for the whole troupe.

Wordiness

Word choice also concerns how succinct or how wordy a piece of text may be. Generally, writers need to avoid wordiness for clear, concise writing. To this end, positive sentences are clearer for readers than negative ones, and dropping common empty phrases like "the fact that," fosters concise writing.

Example: At this moment in time, gas prices have reached an unprecedented high.

Correction: Gas prices today have reached an unprecedented high.

Example: To make a long story short, the perceived global hoarding of oil, which is at a crisis level, is pricing energy beyond the reach of many third world nations.

Correction: The perceived global hoarding of oil, now at crisis levels, is pricing energy beyond the reach of many third world nations.

Example: In spite of the fact that this market report has been compiled for the purpose of educating consumers about choices in alternative energy, no one is listening.

Correction: Although this market report has been compiled to educate consumers about choices in alternative energy, no one is listening.

Idioms (Prepositions)

Idioms are common word constructions that are specific to a language. English has certain idiomatic uses of prepositions, which are tested in the SAT. Below are four common prepositions, their possible uses, and examples:

- in (enclosed within a container or as a point in time or space)
- at (a point in time or space)
- on (as supported on a surface or by words)
- for (a reason for action)

Example: The astronauts will be arriving *in* a Hummer.

Example: The space center will admit visitors *in* one hour.

Example: Military jets are scheduled to await the lift-off *at* the launch site.

Example: Reporters at the site must keep ID tags *on* their cameras.

Example: NASA officials will speak *on* the subject of the shuttle mission.

Example: The junior flight crew is responsible *for* chronicling the journey.

Practice 4: Word Choices

These sentences allow you to assess the correctness and effectiveness of expression. In choosing responses, use the expectations set by standard written English in the area of word choice.

In the sentences below, part of the sentence or the whole sentence is underlined. Beneath these sentences you will find four ways of re-phrasing the underlined part. Choose the response that best expresses the meaning of the original sentence. Choose A if you think the original is correct. Choose one of the others if it is an improvement. Your choice should create the most effective sentence — clear and precise, without awkwardness or ambiguity.

1. The Pentagon cannot hardly ever say it will be completely accurate in its security predictions.
   - A. leave as is
   - B. Pentagon cannot say it will be completely accurate
   - C. Pentagon cannot hardly say it will be completely accurate
   - D. Pentagon hardly never can say it will be completely accurate
   - E. Pentagon ever says it will be completely accurate

2. This summer's heat wave arrived in the western plains of the Rockies during July.
   - A. leave as is
   - B. heat wave arrived for the western plains of the Rockies
   - C. heat wave arrived at the western plains of the Rockies
   - D. a wave of heat arrives on the western plains of the Rockies
   - E. Rockies had a heat wave arrived to the western plains

3. Lewis and Clark experienced the flat plains of Kansas and the peaks of Colorado, and these are the wonders described in their detailed journals.
   - A. leave as is
   - B. detailed in their
   - C. described these wonders in their detailed
   - D. this is the wonder described in their detailed
   - E. Lewis and Clark described them in their detailed

4. He wears his GPS-equipped watch in his wrist with care.
   - A. leave as is
   - B. his GPS-equipped watch at his wrist
   - C. his GPS-equipped watch for his wrist
   - D. his GPS-equipped watch on his wrist
   - E. his GPS-equipped watch to his wrist

5. A well-orchestrated field trip may raise the conscientiousness of students and chaperones.
   - A. leave as is
   - B. field trip may rise the conscientiousness of students
   - C. field trip may raise student consciousness
   - D. field trip may raise the conscience in students
   - E. field trip may raise the consciousness of students

Student Resources: Web Sites and Books

Improving Sentences

http://owl.english.purdue.edu/

The Purdue On-line Writing Center is the bedrock of the site. There are numerous printable hand-outs and lessons. The sections on writing sentences and paragraphs will be a valuable tool for students who enjoy working on-line.

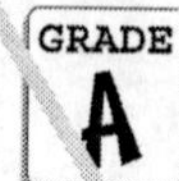

http://bartleby.com/usage

Part of a massive nonprofit resource site, this section offers exhaustive materials for every aspect of writing and editing, from grammar and usage pages to links discussing style and voice. The built-in search engine allows the user to zero in on a topic.

http://www.dictionary.com

This one's name says it all — type a word in its engine and this free site gives you all possible meanings and even some etymology (word history) thrown in for good measure. Look closely for the small function keys beneath the engine blank that allow you to toggle between dictionary, thesaurus, and encyclopedia functions.

Books

Andrea Lunsford. The St Martin's Handbook: With 2003 MLA Update. 5th ed. New York: Bedford St. Martin's, 2003.

A popular textbook in freshman English courses and high schools alike, this most recent edition contains chapters on reading and note-taking, grammar, research, and citation, as well as improving your writing style by avoiding chichés and other common mistakes.

Chapter 6 Review

The test items in this review allow you to assess the correctness and effectiveness of expression. In choosing responses, use the expectations set by standard written English in the areas of grammar, punctuation, sentence construction, and word choice.

In the sentences below, part of the sentence or the whole sentence is underlined. Beneath these sentences you will find four ways of re-phrasing the underlined part. Choose the response that best expresses the meaning of the original sentence. Choose A if you think the original is correct. Choose one of the others if it is an improvement. Your choice should create the most effective sentence — clear and precise, without awkwardness or ambiguity.

1. Indoor plants, whether stately palms, meek fichus trees, prickly Christmas cacti, or fragile ferns, need constant and vigilant care for health and bloom.

   A. leave as is
   B. whether stately palms; meek fichus trees; prickly Christmas cacti; or fragile ferns
   C. whether stately palms, meek fichus trees, cacti, or ferns
   D. whether stately palms, meek fichus trees, prickly Christmas cacti, fragile ferns
   E. whether they are stately palms, meek fichus trees, prickly Christmas cacti, and also fragile ferns

2. Voltaire's masterpiece, *Candide* strips pretense from all social institutions.

   A. leave as is
   B. masterpiece *Candide* strips pretense from
   C. masterpiece, *Candide*, strips pretense from
   D. masterpiece *Candide*; strips pretense from
   E. masterpiece called *Candide* strips pretense from

3. Music storage technology, like other revolutionary technologies, are generated from previous inventions and knowledge.

   A. leave as is
   B. like them of other revolutionary technologies, are generated
   C. like those other revolutionary technologies, are generated
   D. like other revolutionary technologies pertaining to computers, is generated
   E. like other revolutionary technologies, is generated

4. Most orchestra leaders agree that foreign language students not being allowed to express themselves through music, this puts them at a disadvantage with other students.

   A. leave as is
   B. the lack of musical expression foreign language students experience puts
   C. foreign language students hardly not being allowed to express themselves through music puts
   D. when foreign language students who have not been allowed to express themselves through music, it puts
   E. foreign language students allowed expression through music, puts

5. The tsunami of 2004 may have faded from news stories, but efforts are still proceeding on the behalf of victims.
   - A. leave as is
   - B. may have faded from news stories. Efforts, proceed on
   - C. may have faded from news stories: but efforts are still proceeding on
   - D. may fade from news stories but efforts still proceed on
   - E. may have faded from news stories; since efforts are still proceeding on

6. For example, shopping at low-cost neighborhood book stores.
   - A. leave as is
   - B. People can do shopping at low-cost neighborhood book stores for example
   - C. People are turning from "big box stores"; for example, they are shopping at low-cost neighborhood book stores
   - D. For example, shopping at low-cost neighborhood book stores which is popular now
   - E. For example; shopping at low-cost, neighborhood book stores

7. The fact that symptoms of lethal arsenic poisoning mimic those of deadly cholera allowed numerous eighteenth century murders to go undetected by authorities.
   - A. leave as is
   - B. The symptoms of lethal arsenic poisoning mimic deadly cholera, which allowed
   - C. After the fact that symptoms of arsenic poisoning mimic deadly cholera, allowing
   - D. Since symptoms of lethal arsenic poisoning often mimic those of deadly cholera,
   - E. The fact that symptoms of lethal arsenic poisoning mimic deadly cholera allows

8. Traditional downtown parades bring needed droves of tourists, because they are family-oriented events communities offer valuable incentives to any business which will sponsor popular floats.
   - A. leave as is
   - B. tourists because they are family-oriented events
   - C. tourists; because they are family-oriented events,
   - D. tourists since they are family-oriented events,
   - E. tourists: since families are oriented to the events

9. On our hike up Bridal Veil trail, gallons of bottled water were carried by three patient brown burros borrowed from the Grand Canyon tours.
   - A. leave as is
   - B. three patient brown burros, borrowed from the Grand Canyon tours, carried gallons of bottled water
   - C. gallons of bottled water were carried by three patient brown burros, borrowed from the Grand Canyon tours
   - D. gallons of bottled water borrowed from the Grand Canyon tours were carried by three patient brown burros
   - E. three patient brown burros were carried by gallons of bottled water borrowed from the Grand Canyon

10. Few of the pets felt any apparent anxiety as its owners boarded the plane.
    A. leave as is
    B. Few pets felt anxiety as its owner's
    C. Few of the pets, in fact, felt any apparent anxiety as its owners
    D. Few of the pets felt any anxiety as they owners
    E. Few of the pets felt any apparent anxiety as their owners

11. Public radio has established a strong listener base, it provides in-depth reporting, educational enrichment, and the beloved "Bach's Lunch" program.
    A. leave as is
    B. has established a strong listener base: where it provides in-depth reporting
    C. has established a strong listener base, since it provides in-depth reporting
    D. has established a strong listener base; it provides in-depth reporting
    E. has established a strong listener base. Providing in-depth reporting

12. The choral members rose from its chairs to sing a glorious version of Handel's Messiah.
    A. leave as is
    B. The choral members rose from their chairs to sing
    C. Singing, the choral members rose from its chairs for
    D. The choral members rose from it's chairs to sing
    E. Members of the choral rose from its chairs to sing

13. The enclosed letter is sent to call your attention to the fact that the local chapter of the YMCA is sponsoring a community open house for the purpose of strengthening neighborhood activism.
    A. leave as is
    B. sent to call your attention to the fact that the YMCA, local chapter, will sponsor a community open house so to strengthen
    C. sent notifying you about the local chapter of the YMCA sponsoring a community open house for strengthening
    D. about the local chapter, YMCA, sponsoring a community open house for the purpose of strengthening
    E. to call your attention the local chapter of the YMCA, it is sponsoring a community open house for the purpose of strengthening

14. The water in the Dead Sea is being lost through evaporation, by the unceasing presence of wind and sun as well as drawn out by greedy tourists in the area.
    A. leave as is
    B. The water in the Dead Sea which is being lost through evaporation by the unceasing presence of wind and sun as well as drawn out by greedy tourists
    C. The unceasing presence of wind and sun as well as that which is drawn out by greedy tourists, the water in the Dead Sea is being lost through evaporation.
    D. The water in the, Dead Sea, is being lost through evaporation by the unceasing presence of wind and sun as well as drawn out by greedy tourists
    E. The unceasing presence of wind and sun and greedy tourists is causing the loss of water in the Dead Sea

15. Republican Senators and the president must agree on their platforms for the upcoming national election.

    A. leave as is
    B. Republican Senators, and the president, must agree on his platforms
    C. Republican Senators and the president must agree on his platforms
    D. Republican Senators, and the president must agree in his platforms
    E. Republican Senators or the president must agree on their platform

16. The philosophy and goal of yoga is to quiet the mind; to be focusing on the present; to make time for your spirituality; and to experience the "pretzel-ness" of being.

    A. leave as is
    B. yoga is to quiet the mind; to be focusing on the present; to make time for your spirituality; and to experience the "pretzel-ness"
    C. yoga is to quiet minds; to be focusing on presents; for spiritualities: experience "pretzel-nesses"
    D. yoga is to quiet the mind, to focus on the present, to make time for the spiritual, and to experience the "pretzel-ness"
    E. yoga is to: quiet the mind; to be focusing on the present; to make time for the spirituality; and to experience the "pretzel-ness"

Chapter 7
Improving Paragraphs

In addition to the essay, which comprises Section One of the test, the SAT also includes sections which test sentence and paragraph improvement. These sections include questions which test your skills with grammar, punctuation, and sentence structure. Chapter 5 of this book covers many of the skills needed to do well in these sections.

This chapter will focus on the section of the SAT which calls on you to improve the writing and clarity of given paragraphs. As well as issues of grammar and mechanics, these sections address the more fundamental concepts, such as simple clarity of meaning and integrity of structure.

Skills needed for the Paragraph Improvement sections of the SAT are essential not only for performing well in those parts of the test but also for honing your ability to write your own essay for Test Section One of the test. This chapter will give you practice in paragraph writing skills such as the use of **transitions**, the use of **standard English** and **active voice**, and **structure and mechanics** such as proper pronoun reference.

Why improve paragraphs? When you write, your writing will be effective. *How* you communicate your ideas makes all the difference in whether your ideas are heard, understood, taken seriously, and even acted upon. Effective writing changes things: your outlook, other people's minds, or even world events.

To prepare for the SAT Paragraph Improvement sections, we will begin with a sample essay and questions which you will encounter on your test.

Sample Paragraph Improvement Passage

Below is a sample of the kind of passage you will see in the SAT Paragraph Improvement section. It is preceded by the official directions for this section. Become familiar with exactly what these directions say ahead of time, so that you need only scan them at the time of the test. Note that the directions imply that only standard written English is appropriate in college level essays. The Paragraph Improvement section tests your knowledge of — your "ear" for— this form of English.

The standard advice for improving paragraphs is first to read them through carefully for meaning, taking note of anything that sounds awkward or makes you uncomfortable. You will very likely be able to spot these awkward places even if you cannot identify the exact rule or convention that has been broken. This is what is meant for having an ear for language.

Read the following set of directions and the passage. The passage will be used in ensuing sections of the chapter to discuss the three main areas of improvement tested by the Paragraph Improvement section of the SAT. For now, read for meaning, but also be alert for the several errors that the passage contains. You will work with them later in the chapter.

> **Directions:** The following passage is an early draft of an essay. Some parts of the passage need to be rewritten.
>
> Read the passage and select the best answers for the questions that follow. Some questions are about particular sentences or parts of sentences and ask you to improve sentence structure or word choice. Other questions ask you to consider organization and development. In choosing answers, follow the standards of written English.

Sample Passage 1

Before William Caxton set up the first printing press in England in 1476, the only writing available to literate people was hand scripted. They were labor intensive and time consuming products. These manuscripts were relatively few in number. They were accessible to only a small segment of society. They could be read only by the educated classes. Only the nobility and the clergy were literate. All other members of society belonged to the class of laborers and they were generally uneducated and they were known as "commoners." A new merchant class was beginning to emerge in Europe, men who had a basic degree of education, as well as some expendable cash.

The new middle class demanded books, especially good, entertaining stories. Caxton had a receptive market for his product. But what would he print for them? Whatever came from Caxton's press it was bound to have a profound effect on the collective experience, language, and psychology of that society. They were the first "mass produced" writings in Anglo-Saxon society, they were bound to shape culture and ideas.

And they did. One of the early books that came off Caxton's press was Sir Thomas Malory's *Le Morte D'Arthur*. It was unbelievably long. It was originally written in 507 chapters. Malory sat in prison and wrote it as he'd committed a lot of crimes. It was the story of King Arthur and the Knights of the Round Table. It was roughly edited by Caxton himself so that it would be accessible to common people. This story of the great king and his mysterious origin and his beautiful wife, Guenevere and his loyal friend Lancelot, and the noble Knights of the Round Table. It really had a lot to do with the idea of chivalry in the middle ages. Enough romance, mysticism, and adventure was provided by this story to enthrall audiences for hundreds of years. This still beloved story still inspires readers today. On countless occasions this story has been rendered into poem, song, drama, and novel by writers since its first printing.

Another literary work produced by Caxton's press which become a fundamental influence on Anglophone literature and culture is Chaucer's *Canterbury Tales,* first printed in 1476. It consists of stories told by a band of pilgrims. They can still be found in almost every high school and college curriculum in America. They take the reader on a journey to Canterbury in the 14th century. These traveling pilgrims compose entertaining stories that amuse each other while they journey on their pilgrimage. They cover a spectrum of human experience from nunneries to barnyards to the marketplace.

Among the many literary works that came from Caxton's press, *La Morte d'Arthur* and *The Canterbury Tales* illustrate the range of ideas that marked the evolution of literary topics that began to emerge in the late middle ages. Before this time, none of the writers were writing about common people. I think some of the best works of the fantasy genre come from the 20th century. Malory's book was filled with the noble class and great romance and conquest. Chaucer's anthology, on the other hand, caught a glimpse of the middle class and common people's life and foibles. These made for an evolution of literary thought into a form that was written for the people and about the people.

In reading this essay, you came across several parts that were jarring or felt uncomfortable. Pay attention to this feeling when you read Paragraph Improvement passages on the SAT. They usually signal the areas in which the mistakes are made and about which the questions will be asked. Now we will look at the main areas of Paragraph Improvement, using parts of this passage as the samples for each area.

Transitions and the Flow of Ideas

Ideas have to flow smoothly from one to another. Jolting a reader from one idea to the next and leaving the reader to make connections is not a characteristic of good reading. The goal of a reader is to comprehend and analyze ideas, not to figure out what the author could possibly mean by a number of disjointed thoughts. If your car jounced you around on normal roads to the point of giving you a headache, you would have the suspension fixed. In writing, the suspension apparatus needed for a smooth ride consists of techniques such as those listed in the following table.

Transitional Technique	Examples
Using transitional terms	therefore, while, on the other hand, in contrast, furthermore, yet, in spite of, etc.
Using introductory phrases	*By making literature available to common people,* Caxton's press influenced the class structure in British society.
Combining sentences	**(1)** Caxton's press changed the reading habits of common people. **(2)** The reading habits of the common people effected the press by placing greater demand on it. *While Caxton's press changed the reading habits of the common people, that change in the people had a reciprocal effect on the press by placing greater demand on it for more stories.*
Inserting sentences to clarify context	**Unclear**: Only selected segments of society were literate at that time. **Clarified**: *Before Caxton's printing press, hand-scripted texts were relatively rare and had an exclusive readership.* Only selected segments of society were literate at that time.

In testing the use of transitions to augment the smooth flow of ideas, the SAT questions will often be worded:

1. In context, that is, according to the best version of the underlined portions of sentences...
2. Which sentence would be most appropriate to precede sentence number...
3. Which sentence would be most appropriate to follow...
4. In the context, which is the best way to revise and combine the underlined portions of sentences...
5. Which is the best revision to make to a sentence...

Practice Paragraphs: Transitions

The first two paragraphs of the sample passage contain typical mistakes in transitional techniques. Reread the two paragraphs then read the questions pertaining to them. A discussion following the questions explains the answers to the questions.

Excerpt 1 from Sample Passage

(1) Before William Caxton set up the first printing press in England in 1476, the only writing available to literate people was hand scripted. **(2)**They were labor intensive and time consuming products. **(3)**These manuscripts were relatively few in number. **(4)**They were accessible to only a small segment of society. **(5)**They could be read only by the educated classes. **(6)**Only the nobility and the clergy were literate. **(7)**All other members of society belonged to the class of laborers and they were generally uneducated and they were known as "commoners." **(8)**A new merchant class was beginning to emerge in Europe, men who had a basic degree of education, as well as some expendable cash.

(9) The new middle class demanded books, especially good, entertaining stories. **(10)** Caxton had a receptive market for his product. **(11)**But what would he print for them? **(12)** Whatever came from Caxton's press it was bound to have a profound effect on the collective experience, language, and psychology of that society. **(13)**They were the first "mass produced" writings in Anglo-Saxon society, they were bound to shape culture and ideas.

1. In the context, which is the best way to revise and combine sentences 2 and 3? (reproduced below)

   They were labor intensive and time consuming products. These manuscripts were relatively few in number.

   A. leave as is
   B. As they were labor intensive and time consuming products, they were manuscripts that were relatively few in number.
   C. They were labor intensive and time consuming products. They were also relatively few in number.
   D. They were labor intensive and they were time consuming products. These manuscripts were relatively few in number.
   E. As labor intensive and time-consuming products, these manuscripts were relatively few in number.

2. In the context, which is the best way to revise the underlined portions of sentence 7? (reproduced below)

   All other members of society belonged to <u>the class of laborers and they were generally uneducated and they were known as "commoners."</u>

   A. All other members of society belonged to the class of laborers. And they were generally uneducated and they were known as "commoners."
   B. All other members of society belonged to the class of laborers: they were generally uneducated and they were known as "commoners."
   C. All other members of society belonged to the class of laborers who were generally uneducated and they were known as "commoners."
   D. All other members of society belonged to the class of laborers, a generally uneducated class known as "commoners."
   E. All other members of society belonged to the class of laborers, and they were generally uneducated and they were known as "commoners."

3. Which sentence would be most appropriate to precede sentence number 9?
   - A. The new middle class demanded reading material.
   - B. Caxton's import from Germany of Gutenburg's invention began a revolution in literacy.
   - C. Caxton's import from Germany made book production easier.
   - D. The new middle class were primarily merchants and traders.
   - E. The new middle class of people did not like to read hand-scripted texts.

4. Which is the best revision to make to the beginning of sentence 12?
   - A. leave as is
   - B. Whatever comes from Caxton's press it was bound to have a profound effect
   - C. Whatever it was came from Caxton's press it was bound to have a profound effect
   - D. Whatever came from Caxton's press was bound to have a profound effect
   - E. Whatever came from Caxton's press had a profound effect

5. In the context, which is the best way to revise the underlined portions of sentence 13? (reproduced below)

   They were the first "mass produced" writings in Anglo-Saxon society, they were bound to shape culture and ideas.

   - A. leave as is
   - B. As the first "mass produced" writings in Anglo-Saxon society, they were bound to shape culture and ideas.
   - C. They were the first "mass produced" writings in Anglo-Saxon society, being bound to shape culture and ideas.
   - D. As the first "mass produced" writings in Anglo-Saxon society, so they were bound to shape culture and ideas.
   - E. They were the first "mass produced" writings in Anglo-Saxon society, which are bound to shape culture and ideas.

Discussion

The answer to question number 1 is E. The sentences needed to be combined using an introductory phrase: "As labor intensive and time-consuming products..." B sounds as if it might be correct because "As" should not be used in place of "because." If the word "because" were used in B, it would have been an acceptable answer.

The answer to question 2 is D. All other answers use the word "and" inappropriately to string together ideas. "And" should be used to connect two related objects or ideas.

The answer to question 3 is B. This "big picture" statement sets up the reader for the idea that the middle class demanding more literature is part of a revolution in literary accessibility. If you read the other answers carefully, you will see that none of them relates directly to the idea in sentence 9. Ideas in sentences have to relate to ideas in other sentences proximate to them.

The answer to question 4 is D. The only other answer that might appear correct would be E. However, E states a general idea concerning all products from Caxton's press. It says that anything that came from his press would have a profound effect. This might have been true, but nothing in the context of this passage leads the reader to be certain of the truth of that statement. D is the only statement which is grammatically correct and true in the context.

The answer to question 5 is B. Again, B presents a correctly used introductory phrase at the beginning of a simple sentence with a clear subject. The other answers contain mistakes in verb tense or usage.

LANGUAGE AND VOICE

The main issues which the SAT tests in language and voice concern the use of **standard English** and **active voice**. As students of writing, you have heard many times that a written composition should follow the rules of standard English. The use of standard English depends upon the **author's purpose** of the composition. If the composition is formal and informative, the use of standard English is required. If, on the other hand, it is a casual essay meant to entertain, then a more **colloquial**, or informal language is acceptable. That is why some questions will ask you to consider the author's purpose before determining the best language for a paragraph.

Active and **passive voice** pertain to the way an action is described. When a writer describes an action in an active voice, the subject comes first and performs the action: *Jane took the SAT twice*. In contrast, the passive voice focuses on the object of the action first, and then describes the action as what was done to the object: *The SAT was taken by Jane twice*. Conventional standard English for college compositions requires active voice as the preferred mode of expressing ideas. Active voice states a point more directly and effectively that passive voice does. The following table contains some examples of passive and active voice.

Passive	Active
The aria by Puccini was sung by Maria Callas.	Maria Callas sang the aria by Puccini.
The launch of the space shuttle from Cape Canaveral was controlled by N.A.S.A.	N.A.S.A. controlled the launch of the space shuttle from Cape Canaveral.
The test is being prepared for by all 10th grade students in the county.	All 10th grade students in the county are preparing for the test.
An admission of guilt was finally made by the defendant.	The defendant finally made an admission of guilt.

Questions which test the use of language and voice on the SAT are often worded in the following ways:

1. Considering the author's purpose for the essay, which of the following is the best revision of...
2. Which is the best revision of the underlined section of sentence...
3. In the context, which of the following revisions would improve sentence...
4. In the context, which is the best version of sentence...

Other questions testing language and voice will be phrased in a similar way.

Practice Paragraph: Language and Voice

The third paragraph of the main sample passage contains typical mistakes in language and voice. Reread this paragraph, reproduced below, and the questions that follow. A discussion following the questions explains the answers to the questions.

Excerpt 2 from Sample Passage

(1) And they did. **(2)**One of the early books that came off Caxton's press was Sir Richard Malory's *Le Morte D'Arthur.* **(3)**It was unbelievably long. **(4)**It was originally written in 507 chapters. **(5)**Malory sat in prison and wrote it as he'd committed a lot of crimes. **(6)** It was the story of King Arthur and the Knights of the Round Table. **(7)**It was roughly edited by Caxton himself so that it would be accessible to common people. **(8)**This story of the great king and his mysterious origin and his beautiful wife, Guenevere and his loyal friend Lancelot, and the noble Knights of the Round Table. **(9)**It really had a lot to do with the idea of chivalry in the middle ages. **(10)**Enough romance, mysticism, and adventure was provided by this story to enthrall audiences for hundreds of years. **(11)**This still beloved story still inspires readers today. **(12)**On countless occasions this story has been rendered into poem, song, drama, and novel by writers since its first printing.

1. In the context, which of the following revisions would improve sentences 3 and 4? (reproduced below)

   It was unbelievably long. It was originally written in 507 chapters.

   A. Combine the two sentences using a comma.
   B. Change the first sentence to formal language and make the second a subordinate clause.
   C. Add an m-dash between the two sentences and change the first to more formal language.
   D. Combine the sentences using the conjunction "and."
   E. Switch the order of the sentences.

2. Considering the main idea and author's purpose for the essay, which of the following is the best revision of sentence 5? (reproduced below)

   Malory sat in prison and wrote it as he'd committed a lot of crimes.

   A. Leave as is
   B. Malory sat in prison and wrote it: he'd committed a lot of crimes.
   C. Malory sat in prison and wrote it because he'd committed a lot of crimes.
   D. Malory wrote it as he sat in prison, having committed many crimes.
   E. Malory wrote it as he sat in prison because he'd committed a lot of crimes.

3. Which is the best revision of the underlined section of sentences 8 and 9? (reproduced below)

   This story of the great king and his mysterious origin and his beautiful wife, Guenevere and his loyal friend Lancelot, and the noble Knights of the Round Table. It really had a lot to do with the idea of chivalry in the middle ages.

   A. This story of the great king and his mysterious origin, and his beautiful wife, Guenevere, and his loyal friend Lancelot, and the noble Knights of the Round Table, it really had a lot to do with the idea of chivalry in the middle ages.
   B. This story of the great king and his mysterious origin; his beautiful wife, Guenevere, his loyal friend Lancelot; and the noble Knights of the Round Table helped shape the idea of chivalry in the middle ages.
   C. This story of the great king and his mysterious origin; his beautiful wife, Guenevere; his loyal friend Lancelot; and the noble Knights of the Round Table, it helped shape the idea of chivalry in the middle ages.
   D. This story of the great king and his mysterious origin — and his beautiful wife, Guenevere and his loyal friend Lancelot, and the noble Knights of the Round Table — It really had a lot to do with the idea of chivalry in the middle ages.
   E. This story of the great king and his mysterious origin; his beautiful wife, Guenevere; his loyal friend Lancelot; and the noble Knights of the Round Table really had a lot to do with the idea of chivalry in the middle ages.

4. In the context, which is the best version of sentence 12? (reproduced below)

   On countless occasions this story has been rendered into poem, song, drama, and novels by writers since its first printing.

   A. leave as is
   B. On countless occasions, since its first printing, this story has been rendered into poem, song, drama, and novels by writers.
   C. On countless occasions since its first printing, writers have rendered this story into poem, song, drama, and novel.
   D. Since its first printing this story has been rendered into poem, song, drama, and novels by writers on countless occasions.
   E On countless occasions this story, since its first printing, has been rendered into poem, song, drama, and novels by writers.

Discussion

The answer to question #1 is D. The phrase "a lot of" is colloquial and not appropriate for composition. Furthermore, answer B contains a misused colon as well as colloquial language. Answer C contains a misplaced phrase. "Because he'd committed a lot of crimes" is made to sound like the reason he wrote the book. The same phrase, as used in answer E, is ambiguous. It is not clear in this structure if he sat in prison because he'd committed a lot of crimes or if he wrote the book because he'd committed a lot of crimes. In either case, the use of the colloquial language makes this an incorrect choice.

The answer to question #2 is B. It is correct because it does not overuse the conjunction "and," because it contains correct punctuation. The semicolon is necessary in a list in which one of the phrases in the list contains punctuation within itself. In this case, the phrase "his beautiful wife, Guenevere" contains a comma.

Therefore, the entire list (here, of characters in the story) must be punctuated by semicolons. The other answers use the word "and" to connect a string of phrases. This use of "and" is always awkward, and can only be used in rare instances of author's choice for the purpose of having a specific effect.

The answer to question #3 is B. In the original construction, the first sentence contains colloquial language. The original construction also consists of two short sentences beginning with "it," a pronoun with a vague referent (refer to the next section in this chapter on Structure and Mechanics). Pronouns such as "it" should always be used close to the noun they refer to: "**The book** was long, as **it** contained 507 chapters." Answer B is correct because it prescibes a well structured sentence containing an independent clause and *a subordinate clause*: "It was very long, *since it was originally written in 507 chapters*."

The answer to question #4 is C. Answer C is in the active voice ("writers have rendered," rather than "rendered by writers"). It also puts every item in the list (poem, song, drama, etc.) into parallel form, i.e. singular nouns.

STRUCTURE AND MECHANICS

The **structure** of a paragraph refers to the function and shape of a paragraph. To review the structure of a paragraph, refer to **Chapter 4: Writing the Common Essay**. The SAT Paragraph Improvement section will test your understanding of the effectiveness of a paragraph in terms of paragraph sections: topic sentence, body, conclusion, the **unity of the paragraph**, and the **purpose of the paragraph**. Are all sentences in the paragraph relevant? Does the paragraph relate to the purpose the author has for writing it? Does it contain a topic and concluding sentence?

The **mechanics** of writing a paragraph refer to the integrity of language and grammar. To review the grammar aspect of this section, see **Chapter 5: Avoiding Common Errors**. For the purposes of this chapter, we will address two major areas of mechanics tested in the SAT Paragraph Improvement section. They are **pronoun references** and **verb forms**. Pronoun references and verb forms are similar in that they are language structures which depend on other parts of the sentence to determine their correct forms. Pronouns and verbs must agree with other elements in a sentence. Therefore, it is necessary to be aware of exactly what these other sentence elements are determining.

Following is a brief review of the meanings of paragraph unity and paragraph purpose.

Paragraph Unity

A paragraph should present and discuss one topic. The paragraph should contain a topic sentence, body sentences supporting the topic, and a conclusion.

The ideas on the topic should follow logically from one to the next. If a paragraph contains irrelevant material, or takes the reader on confusing leaps from one idea to another without setting context for the next idea, the paragraph unity is weak.

For paragraph unity, look for:

- Is the subject clearly established by a topic sentence or statement?
- Do all sentences in the paragraph support the topic of the paragraph? Do any sentences wander off-topic?
- Is there a clear conclusion to each paragraph's idea?
- Do ideas flow logically from one to the next? Or does one idea simply follow another with no relevance to the train of thought?
- Are ideas introduced that are out of context, and then have to be tied in to the context later in the text?

Paragraph Purpose

The purpose of a paragraph determines how the paragraph is written.

- A paragraph written as part of a formal composition must be written in standard English and follow standard conventions of grammar and usage.
- A paragraph written to entertain or as a purely creative form of writing has a great deal of license with standard English. It may use colloquial language ("slang") and unconventional usage, depending upon the effect the author is trying to create.

Of the above two examples of author's purposes, the second will not be used on the SAT. Therefore, creative writing is not used in this chapter for such a purpose.

The two aspects of mechanics discussed in this chapter are **pronoun reference** and **verb form.**

Pronouns, in composition, refer to nouns. For the sake of clarity, pronouns must be placed as close to those nouns, or **antecedents,** as possible. If there is any ambiguity regarding what the antecedent of the pronoun is, the pronoun should be replaced by the noun it is referring to. Read the following table of examples of correct and incorrect pronoun use.

Incorrect Pronoun Reference	Correct Pronoun Reference
Mismatched antecedent: *Every member* of the drum line hoped that *they* would be chosen as section leader. (*Every* is singular, but the pronoun *they* is plural.)	*Every* member of the drum line hoped that *he or she* would be chosen as section leader.
Vague antecedent: Connor went with his brother Darby to the drum corps show. *He* needed help with the equipment. (The incorrect version is vague as to which brother needed help.)	Connor went with his brother Darby to the drum corps show. He wanted to help Darby with the equipment.
Pronoun far from antecedent: *Darby* arrived at 4:30 to be sure to catch the bus. The corp director, looking groggy, pulled in at 5:00. *He* waved a greeting much too vivacious for that time of day! (Implies that the groggy director waved vivaciously. This would be contradictory and is not what was meant in the description of the event.)	**Darby** arrived at 4:30 to be sure to catch the bus. The corp director, looking groggy, pulled in at 5:00. **Darby** waved a greeting much too vivacious for that time of day!
Ambiguous antecedent: *The buses* full of *students* had barely gone five miles before *they* all went to sleep. (It sounds as if the buses went to sleep.)	The buses full of students had barely gone five miles before the students all went to sleep.
Unclear referents for demonstrative pronouns (this, these, those, etc.): The bus ride was long and uncomfortable, depriving Darby of any real rest. *This* made Darby tired but did not take away his enjoyment of the competition. (Demonstrative pronouns should not stand on their own, but should be followed by specific referents.)	The bus ride was long and uncomfortable, depriving Darby of any real rest. *This aspect of drum corps life* made Darby tired but did not take away his enjoyment of the competition.

The most common SAT questions regarding verb forms have to do with **verb number**: whether the verb is to be singular or plural. Verbs must agree with their subjects, and in most cases it's easy to see whether a subject is singular or plural, and to make the verb agree. However, there are many instances when this assessment is not clear. For these events, some basic rules must be remembered.

Rule	Example
When two nouns or pronouns are joined by "or" the verb number is **singular**.	Either Jane or Joe *is* (not "are") expected to complete the stage set by 6:00.
When two nouns or pronouns are joined by "and" the verb is **plural**.	Both the offense and the defense *work* (not (works") hard in their training
When two singular nouns or pronouns are connected by "neither... nor" or "either... or" the verb is **singular**.	Neither Jim nor Nolan *knows* (not "know") the answer.
When two nouns or pronouns are connected by "neither... nor" or "either... or" and one is singular and one plural, *the one closest to the verb governs the verb number.*	Either Joe's friends or he *is* (not "are") planning the bird watching tour up the coast
These **indefinite pronouns** take a **singular verb**: anyone, everyone, someone, no one, nobody, none, each	None of the orchestra members *has* (not "have") received the new music yet.

Paragraph Practice: Structure and Mechanics

The fourth and fifth paragraphs of the main sample passage contain typical mistakes in structure and mechanics. Reread these paragraphs, reproduced below, and the questions that follow. A discussion of the answers follows the questions

Excerpt 3 from Sample Passage

(1) Another literary work produced by Caxton's press which become a fundamental influence on Anglophone literature and culture is Chaucer's *Canterbury Tales,* first printed in 1476. **(2)**It consists of stories told by a band of pilgrims. **(3)**They can still be found in almost every high school and college curriculum in America. **(4)**They take the reader on a journey to Canterbury in the 14th century. **(5)**These traveling pilgrims compose entertaining stories that amuse each other while they journey on their pilgrimage. **(6)**They cover a spectrum of human experience from nunneries to barnyards to the marketplace.

(7) Among the many literary works that came from Caxton's press, *La Morte d'Arthur* and *The Canterbury Tales* illustrate the range of ideas that marked the evolution of literary topics that began to emerge in the late middle ages. **(8)**Before this time, none of the writers were writing about common people. **(9)**I think some of the best works of the fantasy genre come from the 20th century. **(10)**Malory's book was filled with the noble class and great romance and conquest. **(11)**Chaucer's anthology, on the other hand, caught a glimpse of the middle class and common people's life and foibles. **(12)**These made for an evolution of literary thought into a form that was written for the people and about the people.

1. In the context of this passage, what structural weakness, if any, does sentence 3 have? (reproduced below)

   They can still be found in almost every high school and college curriculum in America.

   A. no structural weakness
   B. incorrect subject/verb agreement
   C. mismatched pronoun/antecedent: "they" cannot refer to "it."
   D. sentence does not contribute to paragraph unity
   E. Ambiguous pronoun antecedent: antecedent could be "stories" or "pilgrims."

2. In the context of this passage, which is the best way to revise sentence 6? (reproduced below)

   They cover a spectrum of human experience from nunneries to barnyards to the marketplace.

   A. leave as is
   B. This collection of stories covers a spectrum of human experience from nunneries to barnyards to the marketplace.
   C. This collection of stories cover a spectrum of human experience from nunneries to barnyards to the marketplace.
   D. They all cover a spectrum of human experience from nunneries to barnyards to the marketplace.
   E. Each cover a spectrum of human experience from nunneries to barnyards to the marketplace

3. Which is the best way to revise sentence 8? (reproduced below)

   Before this time, none of the writers were writing about common people.

   A. leave as is
   B. None of the writers were writing about common people before this time.
   C. Before this time, none were writing about common people.
   D. Before this time, none of the writers was writing about common people.
   E. Before this time, each writer was not writing about common people.

4. Sentence (7) (reproduced below) fulfills which function in the structure of a paragraph?

   Among the many literary works that came from Caxton's press, La Morte d'Arthur and The Canterbury Tales illustrate the range of ideas that marked the evolution of literary topics that began emerging in the late middle ages and 15th century.

   A. Establishes the topic of the paragraph
   B. Repeats the topic of the paragraph
   C. Supports the thesis of the passage
   D. Disrupts the unity of the paragraph by being irrelevant
   E. Supports the topic of the paragraph

5. Considering the purpose of the passage, which is the best way to deal with sentence 9? (reproduced below)

   I think some of the best works of the fantasy genre come from the 20th century.

   A. Revise it so that verb number agrees with the subject of the sentence
   B. Use more formal language
   C. Use specific examples to support the statement
   D. Omit the sentence
   E. Revise it so that pronouns refer clearly to antecedents

6. In the context, which is the best way to revise sentence 12? (reproduced below)

   These made for an evolution of literary thought into a form that was written for the people and about the people.

   A. Each of these makes for an evolution of literary thought into a form that was written for the people and about the people.
   B. Either Chaucer's or Malory's work makes for an evolution of literary thought into a form that was written for the people and about the people.
   C. These two great works of English fiction made for an evolution of literary thought into a form that was written for the people and about the people.
   D. Pilgrims and kings made for an evolution of literary thought into a form that was written for the people and about the people.
   E. These made for an evolution of literary thought into a form that were written for the people and about the people.

Discussion

1. **The answer to question #1 is E.** Remember that you are asked to consider the question *in the context of the passage*. On its own, the sentence technically has no structural weakness. But following its preceding sentence, it is very confusing. "They" could refer to either a number of stories, or it could refer to a band of pilgrims. Logic says that specific band of pilgrims could not be occupying today's high schools and colleges, but structurally, the sentence itself fails to make that clear.

2. **The answer to question #2 is B.** Like question 1, question two involves a choice of possible antecedents. "They," again, could refer to either pilgrims or stories. To clarify this, the best revision is choice B. It specifies exactly the subject of the sentence instead of using a vague pronoun, "they." Note that choice C is similar, but the verb number is plural: "cover." The verb must be singular since it must agree with "collection," not "stories."

3. **The answer to question #3 is D.** This is an instance of the verb number agreeing with an indefinite pronoun, "none." The verb number in this case must be singular. Note that choice E contains a technically sound sentence, in terms of structure. However, the clash between the positive "each" and the negative "was not" creates awkward syntax.

4. **The answer to question #4 is A.** This complex sentence is the topic sentence of the paragraph. It gives an overview of the point the author intends to make in the paragraph.

5. **The answer to question #5 is D**. This sentence about fantasy genre in the 20th century is irrelevant to the topic of the paragraph and the essay. Its language is also colloquial ("I think"). Given the *purpose* of the passage, which the question alludes to, and which is to inform, colloquial language is inappropriate.

6. **The answer to question #6 is C**. Again, the antecedent for "They" in the original sentence is vague. The sentence is corrected by specifying what the subject is: "These two great works of English fiction."

CHAPTER 7 REVIEW

Below is a practice paragraph improvement essay and directions. First, read the directions. Then read the paragraphs carefully and answer the questions that follow.

Directions: The following passage is an early draft of an essay. Some parts of the passage need to be rewritten.

Read the passage, and select the best answers for the questions that follow. Some questions are about particular sentences or parts of sentences and ask you to improve sentence structure or word choice. Other questions ask you to consider organization and development. In choosing answers, follow the requirement of standard written English.

Sample Passage 2

No noisy, intensive agribusiness here. The farmhouses along two-lane Zurich Road, outside of Sodus in Upstate New York, look like models for a children's book on "Grandpa's farm." The late summer sun glints off silver silos alongside red barns. Often on opposite sides of the road from their farmhouses. Orchards of apple trees display fruit in first blush, and cows take their sweet time crossing roads in front of patient cars and tractors.

Pull up alongside of the huge boulder on the side of the road, however, and you stand before a gateway into another world. It's a world which the local residents have heard about since childhood but rarely paid much attention to. Just as well to avoid it.

A quaint wooden sign beckons the visitor onto a grassy pathway leading to Zurich Bog, a registered National Landmark, owned by the Bergen Swamp Preservation Society of Wayne County, and protected by the National Parks Service. The path is wide and pleasant enough at first. Visitors are gently corralled onto a narrow board walk, a mere three boards wide, lying on the ground and running into a forest. Federal regulation prohibits entering the bog alone, an ominous rule that fuels imagination, even when strictly obeyed. As the path becomes narrower and the vegetation thicker, fantasies of thirsty, unstable soil — quicksand — on either side of the path add to the sense of adventure.

And fantasies they are. Quicksand is a common feature of bogs, but contrary to its nightmarish reputation, created by bad movies, it is not a life-threatening monster. Quicksand is saturated grainy soil that has so much water in it that it cannot support weight. It is like the sand closest to the ocean in which your foot sinks as you enter the water. But quicksand is never very deep. Usually only a few inches in depth, it may be as much as waist deep. But it does not "suck" anything into it. In fact, it is more buoyant than water.

Struggling and moving when caught in quicksand is what forces your feet deeper into it. You may remain safe if you lie prone and rest on the surface until you get help.

Fantasy or not, the vegetation, including carnivorous plants and a wide variety of rare trees and ferns, they make a walk through the bog seem like a trip through a tropical jungle. Five entire unique ecosystems are featured by the Zurich Bog. From the entrance, the visitor first enters a swamp forest. After that comes a bog forest, then an open bog, an upland forest, and finally a floating moor. It takes a couple of hours to fully explore this rich ecosystem, hidden and largely ignored in the middle of quiet countryside south of Sodus, New York.

Emerging into the sunlight of Zurich Road after the bog trek feels like returning to the Real World; but the visitor cannot dismiss the bog adventure as a mere sojourn into Middle Earth. The huge boulder by the side of the road frames an iron plaque reminding all who read it how essential to the "Real World" bogs are. It describes the Zurich Bog, which is three miles long and one mile wide, as a place of "exceptional value" and an example of "the nation's natural heritage." Some of the exceptional value of a bog includes its status as one of the last remaining original wilderness. Hundreds of species of rare and endangered animals and plants are sheltered by it. Bogs also act as carbon traps, taking the poisonous carbon particles out of the air, where they cause tremendous environmental damage.

Bogs, which take thousands of years to evolve, possess another exceptional value. They are realms of freedom for fertile imaginations. They are worlds in which man's laws do not rule. They are places unto themselves, delicate yet formidable, frightening yet beautiful. They cannot be created by man, only destroyed. That is why Zurich Bog is protected, so that it can exist to enthrall many more generations and perhaps, in turn, help protect man from his own deteriorating environment.

1. Which is the best way to improve on the structure of sentences 3and 4 in the first paragraph? (reproduced below)

   The late summer sun glints off silver silos alongside red barns. Often on opposite sides of the road from their farmhouses

   A. Combine the two into once sentence; insert comma after "barns."
   B. Insert an m-dash after the word "barns."
   C. Change the sentences to active voice.
   D. Reverse the order of the two sentences and combine them as a compound sentence.
   E. Correct the pronoun "their" to agree with its antecedent.

2. Which of the following sentences, if any, could be inserted before the last sentence of paragraph 2 to make its meaning clearer? (reproduced below)

   Just as well to avoid it.

   A. Leave as is.
   B. Most of the residents of this part of the country are unaware of the national treasure nestled in the bucolic background of their community.
   C. The people of Zurich, New York are proud of their countryside and welcome visitors who wish to visit it.
   D. Stories of men and horses lost in the mud have earned it the name mud pond; "Devil's Lake," the early Native Americans called it.
   E. Farmers of Zurich township are very protective of their community, and cars parked along Zurich Road run the risk of being "borrowed."

3. Which of the following, if any, is the best way to improve the flow of ideas between sentences 3 and 4 of paragraph 3? (reproduced below)

   The path is wide and pleasant enough at first. Visitors are gently corralled onto a narrow board walk, a mere three boards wide, lying on the ground and running into a forest.

   A. Leave as is.
   B. Begin the first sentence with the adverb "while."
   C. Begin the second sentence with "Also."
   D. Combine the two into one sentence, using a comma and the conjunction "and."
   E. Add the introductory phrase "Before long, however," to beginning of the second sentence.

4. Sentence 4 of paragraph 4 performs which function in adding to the meaning in the paragraph? (reproduced below)

   It is like the sand closest to the ocean in which your foot sinks as you enter the water.

   A. It compares the experience of walking in a bog to the feeling of swimming at the beach.
   B. It presents an example of something like quicksand which many readers have probably experienced in their own lives.
   C. It illustrates that sandy beaches that many readers visit every summer are actually composed of quicksand.
   D. It reassures the reader that the sandy beaches that people experience every summer are not as dangerous as quicksand.
   E. It cautions the reader that being drowned in quicksand is as easy as being drowned in the ocean.

5. In the context, which is the best way to revise the first sentence of paragraph 5? (reproduced below)

   Fantasy or not, the vegetation, including carnivorous plants and a wide variety of rare trees and ferns, they make a walk through the bog seem like a trip through a tropical jungle.

   A. Change the sentence to the passive voice.
   B. Split the sentence into two sentences joined with "and."
   C. Change the sentence to the active voice.
   D. Change "they" to "it."
   E. Delete "they" and change "make" to "makes"

6. Which is the best way to revise sentence 5 in paragraph 6? (reproduced below)

   Hundreds of species of rare and endangered animals and plants are sheltered by it.

   A. Change the sentence to passive voice.
   B. Rewrite the sentence in more colloquial language.
   C. Change the sentence to active voice.
   D. Rewrite the sentence in more formal language.
   E. Leave as is.

Chapter 8
Editing the Essay

Congratulations! You've used your time wisely, carefully read the prompt, brainstormed ideas and formulated supporting evidence. All this work has produced the first draft essay for the SAT.

Now you're ready for the final step: editing and revision. Realistically, you won't have a lot of time to make fine adjustments, perhaps only a minute or two. But remember the time is yours to take advantage of, and every bit helps.

This chapter focuses on editing, not in the sense of making major content changes or drastic alteration, but to provide background information on correcting and fine-tuning the most glaring problems with your essay. These changes can include correcting punctuation and grammar or quickly inserting a clarifying or helpful sentence. By absorbing this material, you'll be able to quickly spot and fix most minor flaws and imperfections.

It may help you to think of your essay as a sculpture. In writing the first draft, you created the clay and gave shape to your creation. Editing involves smoothing out the rough edges and adding shading and detail to your finished work.

Three levels of editing that will be discussed in this chapter:

- **Editing for structure**: organization of essay and of paragraphs (Chapters 1 and 4)
- **Editing for content**: language, point of view (Chapter 2)
- **Editing for mechanics**: grammar, punctuation, usage (Chapter 5)

Editing for Structure

To review the elements of structure in an essay, you will recall the overall essay requires a specific structure, and that the units within the essay — the paragraphs — also require a specific structure. We will look at these two structures separately.

ESSAY STRUCTURE

The structure of the essay consists of three parts:

A quick glance at an essay draft will tell if these three parts are present.

A closer look will reveal if each is effectively performing its function. Following is a checklist of considerations for each essay part. It suggests the kinds of questions to keep in mind when checking the essay structure. Remember, this is simply to give a general idea of factors to keep in mind as you reread. If you notice even one of these factors in your essay and make a change for the better, you've improved your score.

Introduction

- Does it have a strong lead?
- Does it have a clear thesis?
- Does it answer the question?

Body

- Does it consist of at least two paragraphs?
- Does it present relevant points and support them with evidence?

Conclusion

- Does it consist of one paragraph?
- Does it restate the thesis without using exact words?
- Does it give a general summary of the points made in the essay body?
- Does it tie up the ideas with a strong final statement?

Look at the following essay draft and see how many of the above questions come to mind as you read:

Writing Prompt

> Think carefully about the issue in the quotation and the assignment below.
>
> *"This world demands the qualities of youth: not a time of life but a state of mind, a temper of the will, a quality of the imagination, a predominance of courage over timidity, of the appetite for adventure over the love of ease."*
>
> *– Robert F. Kennedy, 1966*
>
> **Assignment**: Do you think young Americans today possess the qualities of youth as described by Robert F. Kennedy?

Essay #1

Intro *(clear thesis, reference to Prompt quote, three points made)*	Young Americans today possess many qualities, but few of the ones described by Robert F. Kennedy as qualities of youth. They don't have a strong will, a predominance of courage, or an appetite for adventure.
First body paragraph *(cites example to support thesis)*	If teens do use a strong will, it is usually to get immediate wishes. Teens who think seriously about the future and try to make it a good one, sometimes making sacrifices for it, are few, and they are often mocked for their behavior. For instance, there is the stereotype of the "nerd." A nerd is a student who might stay home from a party in order to study for a test. That student is a model of good sense. Yet she is also an object of ridicule. The word "nerd," in fact, is recognized as a derogatory term.
Second body paragraph *(cites example to support thesis)*	Look at the self-destructive behavior in teens over the last few decades. Drug use, smoking, drinking, and violence are increasing, even though teens have learned of their destructiveness since kindergarten. It's because of peer pressure. Apparently most teens would rather face a jail sentence than "friends" who want them to behave badly. This is not courage.
Third body paragraph *(cites example to support thesis)*	Teens today like adventure, but usually meaningless adventure. Mr. Kennedy probably thought of adventure as a passion for exploring the world, seeking new knowledge, and learning from people who are not like yourself. Today, teens often confuse this type of adventure with anything that produces an adrenaline rush. Television programs such as "Fear Factor" demonstrate what American youth now consider adventure. I do not think that this is the kind of adventure that Kennedy had in mind.
Conclusion *(no concluding paragraph)*	

While essay #1 has a few weaknesses in language and other details, it is a moderately strong argument with clearly stated points. The structural weakness that stands out in a cursory review of this essay is the **lack of a concluding paragraph**.

It would take only a few seconds to add a couple of sentences as a conclusion to this essay, which might look like this:

Conclusion:	I think Robert F. Kennedy was right when he said the qualities of youth are needed today. But the qualities he describes are rare and, in fact, face extinction in the youth of today.

These two concluding sentences refer back to the prompt as a way of wrapping up its ideas. It restates the thesis to emphasize a connection between the examples cited and the main idea of the essay. It also closes the essay with a strong, unequivocal statement.

PARAGRAPH STRUCTURE

You will recall from **Chapter 1: Writing Paragraphs**, that a paragraph must perform three functions. It must

- state the main idea of the paragraph (topic sentence),
- support the main idea of the paragraph (supporting sentences), and
- tie the main idea of the paragraph into the thesis of the essay (concluding sentence).

Look again at the following paragraph, taken from the preceding essay.

Topic sentence *(underlined)* **Supporting sentences** *(example of "nerd" as derogatory)* **Concluding sentence** *(no conclusion which ties into the main thesis)*	<u>If teens do use a strong will, it is usually to get immediate wishes.</u> Teens who think seriously about the future and try to make it a good one, sometimes making sacrifices for it, are few, and they are often mocked for their behavior. For instance, there is the stereotype of the "nerd." A nerd is a student who might stay home from a party in order to study for a test. That student is a model of good sense. Yet she is also an object of ridicule. The word "nerd," in fact, is recognized as a derogatory term.

The paragraph above gives a good example of the idea that young people mock certain qualities in others. But the paragraph does not specifically apply that example to the thesis of the essay. The part of the thesis addressed in this paragraph is that young people *do not have a strong will*. This idea is stated in the topic sentence of the paragraph. But the evidence given – the idea of the "nerd" as a derogatory quality in teens—is not specifically tied to the main thesis. This can be fixed with one sentence.

Concluding sentence *(shows that the example proves the thesis regarding a lack of strong will in youth.)*	When a person who has the qualities of good judgement and strong will is ridiculed rather than admired by young people, it seems to me that the youth of our country do not value these qualities.

The second body paragraph from the essay also lacks part of its structure. Read the following analysis carefully.

Topic sentence *(no topic sentence)*	
Supporting sentences *(examples of self-destructive behavior in teens)*	Look at the self-destructive behavior in teens over the last few decades. Drug use, smoking, drinking, and violence are increasing, even as teens learn of their destructiveness since kindergarten. It's because of peer pressure. Apparently most teens would rather face a jail sentence than "friends" who want them to behave badly. <u>This is not courage.</u>
Concluding sentence *(underlined)*	

The paragraph above cites examples of self-destructive behavior which continues to be part of many teens' lives. It argues that teens engage in this behavior because of an inability to stand up to peer pressure. It concludes that this weakness shows a lack of courage in teens, which is one of the qualities that Kennedy states is a quality of youth. However, the paragraph does not contain a general topic sentence which tells the reader what the main idea of the paragraph is. Below is a possible topic sentence to fill this need.

Topic sentence	While Mr. Kennedy names courage as a quality of youth, I believe today's youth are sometimes reckless, but not courageous.

A quick survey of each paragraph in your first draft essay can reveal if all three parts are present and effective. If one is lacking, inserting a sentence or a phrase can make a difference in your essay score.

Practice 1: Editing for Structure

A. Read over the following draft of an SAT essay. Name any missing element of the essay structure. Write a possible replacement for the missing part.

Subliminal is Everywhere

I believe that advertisers have a right to insert content advertising into TV shows and movies. In doing so, they are simply exercising their freedom of speech, one of the hallmarks of a democracy. If viewers cannot accept the barrage of brand names placed before them in the entertainment they watch, then they should stay away from that entertainment. There are plenty of other places in which these viewers can happily view advertising that does not seem to bother them.

One area in which our consumer society is swamped with covert advertising is in the apparel industry. Most American teens wear clothes that advertise businesses. Many tee shirts they wear simply splay their designer names blatantly in the front or back, where they are hard to miss. Others act as a billboard for the upscale store where the tee shirts were purchased. Even when these bits of information are not prominently displayed, the styles of the clothes give away the source of the clothes. Teens know which styles reflect which stores. So, if this kind of advertising is acceptable, then why complain about a movie star sipping a Starbucks coffee on screen?

Another area in which advertising is all around us is in the cars we drive. Which item more publicly and loudly advertises who we are and what we value than the cars we drive? Watch the parade of cars driving into the high school parking lot any morning, and you can see anything from beat-up Chevies to this year's Humvee model. If we don't mind driving an advertisement about ourselves, then why complain about the brand name cars used on a television show?

1. Which part is missing?

____

2. Write a possible replacement.

____

____

B. Read the following paragraph from another essay draft. Identify the parts of the paragraph. Then answer the questions that follow.

Paragraph from Essay on Subliminal Advertising

People would not want companies to put hidden ingredients in their foods. They would not want hidden costs added to the clothes they buy. I would not want the college I attend to suddenly charge me extra tuition which they had hidden from me. It's illegal not to disclose to a house buyer that the paint used on your house has lead in it. And companies have been sued by allergy sufferers for not listing peanut products in their snacks. So why would it be acceptable to hide advertising in movies by using subliminal methods?

1. Which part is missing?

____

2. Write a possible replacement.

____

____

Editing for Content

Your essay's content is made up of everything you say within the essay, and **editing for content** involves making sure you've said what you want clearly and with consistency. Editing an SAT essay draft for content involves efficiently checking the two main aspects of persuasive writing: the **argument** and the **evidence**. Remember, your paper takes a position (your argument) and then defends it (with evidence). As such, ask yourself these questions when rereading:

Argument

- Is my argument clearly stated?
- Does my argument keep the same opinion throughout the essay?

Evidence

- Is the evidence present in each point made within the body paragraphs?
- Does the essay present concrete examples to back up my position?
- Is all the evidence relevant to the thesis statement of the essay?

Reviewing the Argument

As you learned in **Chapter 4: Writing the Opinion Essay** you must form one argument, state it clearly, and maintain it consistently throughout the essay. The example essay #1 on page 135 demonstrates a clearly stated, unambiguous argument. It is: "*Young Americans today possess many qualities, but few of the ones described by Robert F. Kennedy as qualities of youth.*" The rest of the essay cites examples which support this opinion.

Remember, you are writing a persuasive essay that supports a point of view, and not a *narrative*, which merely relates a series of events. In this respect, your opinion is important, even crucial. Read the following four opening paragraphs, comparing their lack of *perspective* (or point of view) in the first two with the more opinionated examples that follow.

Simple Narrative

I hope to work for a nonprofit organization, Fair Trade™, after college. I plan to get a degree in psychology, and then to see what the rest of the world is like. I want to help set up cooperative schools for organic coffee growers in Mexico, so that their children can be educated and get out of poverty.

Simple Description

The quality of courage can take many forms. It is not always about facing enemies. Courage can sometimes mean pushing yourself beyond your comfort zone. It can be about learning new things. Sometimes it takes courage to let go of your own ideas and accept other ideas as also being valid. Courage ultimately can mean the ability to live with uncertainty.

Narrative as Argument

<u>I believe that I possess the youthful qualities of courage and love of adventure</u>. I plan to work for a nonprofit organization, Fair Trade™, after college. I want to get a degree in

psychology, and then to see what the rest of the world is like. I want to help set up cooperative schools for organic coffee growers in Mexico, so that their children can be educated and get out of poverty. These dreams are not prompted by a "love of ease," but rather an idealism and courage to try to make the world a little better. They are the qualities that Kennedy called for.

Description as Argument

To see the qualities of youth in today's teens, one has to look closely at the meanings of those qualities. For example, the quality of courage can take many forms. It is not always about facing enemies. Courage can sometimes mean pushing yourself beyond your comfort zone. It can be about learning new things. Sometimes it takes courage even to be able to let go of your own ideas and accept other ideas as also being valid. Courage ultimately can mean the ability to live with uncertainty. For teens to even find their own way and keep their own truths in this age of limitless ideas and information, they must possess great courage.

Adding one or two short sentences can change the weak narratives into a strong argument. As you reread your own essay, ask yourself if you have stated one opinion and maintained it throughout.

Reviewing for Evidence

Once you have established that your opinion has been stated in each paragraph, check to see that you have included at least one piece of evidence per paragraph to support the argument. This evidence must be **relevant** and **specific**.

Read the following paragraphs which compare evidence that is relevant and specific with that which is neither.

Irrelevant

Young people today are needed more than ever to fight for their country. There are also many advantages to joining the military, including job training and education.

Relevant

Young people continue to join the armed forces to defend their country, in spite of the certainty of being deployed to a war zone and fighting the kind of battles no training can really prepare them for. This takes courage.

Vague

Some young people with promising futures sacrifice those futures to become part of their country's defense and to liberate the oppressed.

Specific

Distinguished NFL player Pat Tillman proudly left a great career in football to join the military. He died for his country in Afghanistan in 2004.

Check your essay to ensure that all of your evidence is both relevant and specific.

Practice 2: Editing for Content

The following paragraphs present an argument with some weak evidence. Underline the sentence or sentences that state the argument. Then decide why the evidence is weak. On a separate sheet of paper, write if the evidence is general or irrelevant. Then, suggest an alternative expression of the evidence to make it relevant and specific. The prompt for these paragraphs is the following:

Writing Prompt

> Think carefully about the issue in the quotation and the assignment below.
>
> *The scientific theory of brain hemisphere functions entails the idea that almost all people use more of one side of the brain than the other. Simply put, if people use the left hemisphere of the brain, they tend to be literal, mathematical, logical people. They do well with understanding facts and ideas. If they use the right side of the brain more, they tend to be creative, intuitive people. They deal well with making connections and seeing relationships between facts and ideas.*
>
> **Assignment**: Is it better to be a right-brained or a left-brained person in the 21st century?

Paragraph 1

It is better to be a left-brained person in the 21st century if you want to thrive in this culture. Left brained people can absorb all the information available in this century. Information today is ubiquitous. Computers have made information available to everyone at the click of a mouse. For this reason, it is hard to shelter young people from inappropriate information. However, some countries have tried to filter the barrage of Internet information from their people. For instance, the government of China controls the servers available to Chinese people, and those servers have access to only government approved sites. The Chinese government does this to control the minds of its citizens. They think they can control the growth of knowledge and ideas, but I do not think this is possible forever, when human beings are involved.

Paragraph 2

Left-brained people find the relationship and connections between ideas. They can therefore come up with new ideas from these relationships. They can create new ideas for society. Therefore, I believe it is better to be a left-brained person in the 21st century if you want to make this world a better one. Ideas are good to have, but people have to go beyond ideas to bring new things into existence. If new ideas are not generated, then knowledge would stop. If right brained people can bring in new ideas to make the world better, then it is better to be right brained person today. The world needs new ideas. Some of the greatest people in the history of civilization have been the creative ones, the ones that see the way things are, make connections between ideas, and come up with something better. I believe that it is better to be a left-brained person today.

EDITING FOR LANGUAGE AND GRAMMAR

Many of the skills used in editing your essay for grammar, punctuation, spelling and usage are outlined in **Chapter 5: Avoiding Common Errors**. A careful reading of that chapter will help you to avoid the most common errors in your first draft. This section will focus on **language**, **grammar**, and **sentence structure**. That is because, with a few minutes to look over your draft, you may be able to make slight changes in these areas to improve your score.

The paragraphs in this section are written in response to the following prompt and assignment:

Writing Prompt

Think carefully about the issue in the quotation and the assignment below.

Some champions of the Right to Life movement are advocating a law which permits pharmacists to opt out, on moral grounds, of selling certain birth control pills because they feel it causes a loss of a fetus' life. Other citizens feel that it is a right of an individual to fill a prescription given by a doctor, regardless of the personal views of the pharmacist.

Assignment: Does the government have the right to coerce a professional of any kind to fulfill certain duties of that profession even when doing so would violate the personal values of that professional?

LANGUAGE

You use colloquialisms every day when speaking with your friends, but remember the SAT essay is graded on mastery of standard English. Keep this in mind while scanning over your writing. If your writing includes words or phrases you'd use on the phone, it's probably too colloquial (too "slangy") for the SAT.

Below are examples of sentences written in colloquial language:

1. I'm kind of against laws that make people go against their beliefs.
2. Think about it. Why did this guy choose this profession anyway?
3. I mean, there is always someone who will give you your prescription.
4. It's like, no government should be able to tell me what to do in my job.
5. It's nice to have personal values and all, but you got to do your job, too.

Consider the previous examples when changed into standard English — that is, having had all colloquialisms removed.

1. I do not support laws which make people deny their own beliefs.
2. Why would someone choose the profession of pharmacist in the first place?
3. A patient can usually find a pharmacist willing to fill her prescription.
4. I do not believe the government should have the right to dictate my professional duties.
5. Personal values are positive attributes, but a person must fulfill professional obligations.

As you can see, standard English is both more forceful and more formal, without the qualifications ("kind of," "like," "It's nice ...and all, but") that make up daily conversation. That's not to say it's stuffy — far from it — but there's a structure and format to standard English that our daily speech lacks.

GRAMMAR

The two aspects of grammar discussed in this section are two of the most common areas of confusion in writing correct sentences: **verbs** and **pronouns**. The primary concerns in both is *form* and *agreement*. Verbs and pronouns must both have the correct form (tense and person) and agreement with the subject they are linked to (in number, singular or plural).

VERBS

Most questions in the SAT sections on sentence improvement and paragraph improvement have to do with **verbs**. The two aspects of verbs that are most important to check for are **verb tense** and **subject verb agreement**. Verbs agree with subject by being the same number, i.e. singular or plural, as their subjects. Below are some sample sentences in which verbs have the incorrect tense or do not agree with their subjects. The corrected term follows each sentence in parentheses.

Subject/verb agreement	Tense
• A profession like pharmacy are essential for everyone's health. (*A profession...* is) • Neither of them have the right to deny service. (*Neither...* has) • None of the other professions have as many moral questions to face as medicine has. (*None...* has) • Doctors have always faced moral dilemmas, but only recently has the ethics of chemistry become so crucial to pharmacists. (have *the ethics*) • There is usually two or more pharmacists to attend to a patient in most pharmacies. (There are... *two* or more)	• Airline pilots logged thousands of air miles before they begin flying commercial jets. (Airline pilots have logged...) • Because ethics is an important part of medicine, medical schools included ethics courses in their curriculum. (include) • When she graduated last year, my doctor has completed at least one course in ethics. (had completed) • Laws have always governed professions that have involved public safety. (involve) • While I was listening to the radio, I hear a story about a pharmacist who lost her job because she refused a customer. (I heard)

Pronoun/Antecedent Agreement

One of the most devious infiltrations of colloquial English into standard written English is the invasion of the vague or incorrect pronoun/noun agreement. When we write the way we talk, we are often unclear about who or what we are referring to when we use pronouns. We will also sometimes mistake whether the pronoun is singular or plural. But in writing, the agreement between a pronoun and the noun it refers to (antecedent) must be very clear.

Every pronoun refers to a noun or subject. Since pronouns take the place of nouns or subjects, they must have the same number (singular or plural) as the nouns or subjects they replace. They must also have the same person (first person, second person, third person). Consider the following sentences in which the pronoun does not agree with its antecedent.

1. In college, it's important for each student, in spite of all the distracting influences everywhere, to remember to do their homework. (**Number**. Change to *his* or *her* to agree with *student*.))
2. If someone wants to write well, it's almost as if you have to learn two different languages: speaking English and written English. (**Person**. Change to *he* or *she* to agree with *person*. Don't forget to change *have* to *has*.)
3. Anyone can learn to rappel, provided they are not afraid of heights. (**Number**. Change *they* to *he* or *she* to agree with *anybody* (singular) Don't forget to change *are* to *is*.
4. Either football or orchestra will find that their funds have been cut for next year. (**Number**. Change *their* to *its* agree with the singular produced by *either... or*.)
5. No one could bring themselves to be the first to leave. (**Number**. Change *themselves* to *himself* or *herself*.)

Two notes on avoiding pronoun/antecedent traps:

1. The following indefinite pronouns are always singular and always take a singular pronoun: everyone, everybody, no one, no body, anyone, any body. (See example questions 3 and 5 above.)
2. When you need a third person singular pronoun (*he, she, him,* or *her*) and you are concerned about which gender to choose, remember that it is now an acceptable convention to choose one or the other. It is not necessary to always use the unwieldy "he or she" or "him or her."

Punctuation

The SAT essay graders understand that the essay is a first draft written under time constraints. They also know that the essay tests a student's ability to present ideas in a clear and organized way. While the graders are not meticulous about punctuation, There are some major punctuation issues that may affect your score While reading over your essay, look for these red flags:

- Always capitalize the first word of each sentence.
- Make sure all periods — and other end punctuations — only come after **complete** sentences.
- Make sure your possessive nouns and pronouns contain an apostrophe (except for **its**, as in **the dog could not catch its tail**).
- Underline the titles of books, movies, plays, poems, and short stories you refer to in your essay. Use quotation marks when referring to written articles.

Practice 3: Editing for Language, Grammar, and Punctuation

The following two paragraphs contain errors in **language**, **grammar**, and **punctuation**. Read the paragraphs carefully and, on a separate sheet of paper, rewrite them with corrections.

When the government goes and tells people how to do their jobs, they took away their right to practice religion. A health professional cant be told how they had to act morally. The concept of civil disobedience was an example of how the law of right and wrong are higher than civil law. People who practiced civil disobedience, such as Martin Luther King, do so because he believed in their own conscience more than in civil laws. Of course, they take their punishment because they respected the law but they follow their own law of right and wrong first. Therefore, neither government nor law enforcement have the right to make a worker to act against their conscience.

It is important for the government to regulate each profession as far as their safety standards are concerned. Like you wouldn't want a restaurant to be filthy. Or the food to be stored improperly. In his book The Jungle, Upton Sinclair showed the need for the government to regulate their citizens safety and protect their rights. that was almost a hundred years ago. Will the government regulation of this century be of a workers conscience? That would be dumb. Each professional can make up their minds as to what is the moral thing to do. If a pharmacist doesn't want to dispense a pill that will kill a fetus, then you shouldn't have to do it. Even if you're the last pharmacist around!

Chapter 8 Review

A. Below is an SAT essay written in 20 minutes or less. It contains errors pertaining to structure and language. Make changes to the essay on the extra space between each line of text. **Hint:** one part of the essay structure as a whole is missing. Check the answer key to see if you caught every error.

Writing Prompt

Think carefully about the issue in the quotation and the assignment below.

> *School boards in at least two states, Georgia and Nebraska, have attempted to impose a curriculum change onto science teachers in their districts. They have attempted to mandate the inclusion of creationism into biology courses. Creationism is a teaching, based in religion, that God created the universe. Scientists maintain that creationism cannot be supported by the same scientific methods that other scientific teaching is supported by. However, some school boards feel that teachers should present both theories of the development of life on earth, evolution and creationism, to their students.*

Assignment: Should governments be able to mandate how and what scientists teach to their classes?

KISS: Keep It Simple and Separate

America is the land of free speech and the pursuit of happiness and the free pursuit of knowledge. To answer a question regarding the role of government in the teaching of science, you have to define the overall role of a democratic government, of science, and of religion in our lives. I think government got to take care of people physically. And science is meant to find knowledge. And religion gives you freedom of faith. None of them need to get mixed up with the others.

It would be awful if government, including school boards which are elected, decided to make all the teachers in it's schools become members of, say, the Methodist church. History has shown that this sort of government mixing up with people's religions turns out awful. For instance, look at Afghani women being killed by the Taliban for not wearing religious scarves! OK, that example is pretty brutal, but hey, it shows what can happen.

Now, science is the pursuit of knowledge. In order to be OK, that knowledge has to be tested in the same way as all scientific knowledge. Science shouldn't be used to promote beliefs—unless those beliefs can hold up to the same tests that science is. Think about it. in the early 20th century, white supremacists tried to use science to prove that non-white people were genetically inferior. It turns out to be full of holes of course. but don't use science that way.

Finally, science teachers should be respected. As professionals. They know their stuff. Better than members of school boards, unless they are all biologists. My cousin is on a school board. And he's an English major. Therefore, government should listen to science teachers. Instead of telling them what to teach. And if science teachers feel it is against their principles, they shouldn't have to do it. I mean, just as a pharmacist should be allowed to follow their consciences when dispensing medicines, science teachers should, too.

B. The following three paragraphs are taken from an essay written to the above prompt. Each paragraph contains errors pertaining to grammar and punctuation. Make changes to the essay on the extra space between each line of text. Check the Answer Key to see if you caught every error.

From: "There's Always Math"

Society is build on more than knowledge. And laws. It is also built on principles. If a government has no right to safeguard the principles on which it's country is built, than who is going to do it? Besides, the government is where the money for schools come from. I think that government provides education for their citizen's and therefore should have a say in what that education consists in.

I think it is a question of ownership. Who is responsible for the education we received? From the time we enter kindergarten to the time we graduated from high school? in the United States the government was. They had begun public education and they pay for it through collecting taxes. Therefore, they are responsible to it. Therefore, they should be able to tell them what to teach.

People say that teacher's should only teach fact's and not try to teach belief's or ideas that come from religion. Yet we are doing those everyday. Each student, regardless of the religion they practice, are expected to learn the "character word of the week" since kindergarten. we teach values all the time. besides its a matter of choice. Alls the teachers have to do is teach both creationism and evolution. That way the student could choose what is right for them. And if the teacher doesn't want to teach both. They can always become a math teacher. Math you can't argue with.

I believe that just teaching the theory of evolution cheats American students. We already teach both information and values. Teaching creationism might could just bring a feeling of just how awesome this universe is back into students' heads. thus keeping our society humble and strong.

Chapter 9
Neophytes' Guide to Scoring SAT Essays

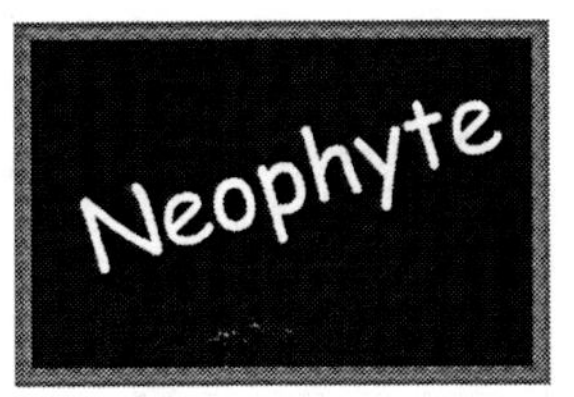

Do you believe you're a neophyte? Have your writing skills just begun to grow? "Neophyte" comes from the Latin word *neophytus*, meaning "newly planted." The English derivation has come to mean a beginner, someone new to a process or skill. Your skills as an SAT writer are taking shape with each practice essay you write.

Asking students to score essays is taking them out of their native soil, into the work normally done by a teacher. But in learning the essay grading process, you can anticipate the scorers' reactions to your work and form strategies to get the best possible grade.

In this chapter, you will learn several aspects of scoring SAT essays:

- **how SAT essays** are scored with the **Scoring Guide**;
- **what SAT readers** expect in a successful essay; and
- **how you can write** a successful essay.

Several essays are provided so you may use the scoring guide to rate essays on your own. With this practice, you will be better able to recognize the elements of a successful essay in your own writing. This is not a timed event, so you won't need a stopwatch.

TIP

When scoring the essays, keep in mind that the readers value a strong, consistent opinion and clear organization with relevant supporting evidence more than perfect punctuation or spelling. Some errors are seen as acceptable in those areas, as long as they do not interfere with the essay's logic.

How are SAT Essays Scored?

The SAT essays are reviewed according to a standard **Scoring Guide**, made from a list of expectations given by professional readers. The following guide is a summary of the one used by SAT readers and lists the requirements of each score (from 0 to 6, with 6 the highest).

SAT Scoring Guide

An essay which scores a 6 is a *superior* essay displaying a mastery of writing skills. It may have some insignificant errors that do not interfere with the essay logic. Score 6 essay elements are:

- a clearly formed opinion on the issue with superior critical thinking using logical examples, suitable reasons, and other supporting evidence
- effective organization and consistent focus, as well as logically flowing transitions and essay unity
- a clear understanding of word usage, including word variety and appropriate word choice
- a variety of sentence structures which add to the essay's flow of ideas and pace
- few errors in grammar, usage, and mechanics

An essay which scores a 5 is a *successful* essay displaying a fairly reliable level of writing skills mastery. It may have a few significant errors that interfere with the essay's logic. Score 5 essay elements are:

- a clearly formed opinion on the issue displaying a high level of critical thinking, using logical examples, suitable reasons, and other supporting evidence for the opinion
- clear organization and focus on the opinion as well as smooth transitions and unity within the essay
- an understanding of word usage, with appropriate word choice
- a variety of sentence structures
- uses mostly correct grammar, usage, and mechanics

An essay which scores a 4 is a *passing* essay which displays some mastery of writing skills. It will have some significant errors which interfere with the logic of the essay. Score 4 essay elements are:

- an opinion on the issue displaying acceptable critical thinking by using satisfactory examples, reasons, and other supporting evidence for the opinion
- satisfactory organization and focus on the opinion as well as some transitions and unity within the essay
- an unreliable understanding of word usage, using some appropriate word choices
- some variety in sentence structures
- a number of errors in grammar, usage, and mechanics

An essay which scores a 3 is a *deficient* essay and displays an early stage of mastery over writing skills. It will have one or more of the following significant errors:

- forms an opinion on the issue displaying some critical thinking, using few or ill-chosen examples, reasons, and other evidence for the opinion
- little evidence of organization and focus, but has gaps in logical flow with missing transitions and some disjointed ideas
- displays an early stage in understanding of word usage, with some variety but uses some inappropriate word choices
- uses repetitive sentence structures which interfere with pace and tone
- contains numerous errors in grammar, usage, and mechanics

An essay which scores a 2 is a *gravely deficient* essay displaying slight mastery of writing skills. It will have multiple significant errors:

- an unfocused opinion (point of view) on the issue, displaying feeble critical thinking, using illogical or too few examples, unsuitable reasons, and hardly any other evidence for the opinion
- lack of organization and deficient in focus, displaying few transitions and a disjointed progression of ideas
- grave misunderstanding of word usage, using basic vocabulary and incorrect word choice
- very limited skill with sentence structures
- numerous errors in grammar, usage, and mechanics, interfering with the essay's logic

An essay which scores a 1 is a *thoroughly unsuccessful* essay displaying practically no mastery of writing skills. It will have multiple significant errors:

- no opinion given on the issue, or one given on unrelated topic; displays a lack of critical thinking as slight or no appropriate support is given
- unorganized and unfocused, having no logical progression and no unity in essay
- pervasive difficulties with vocabulary and word choice
- deficient sentence structures
- numerous errors in grammar, usage, and mechanics, interfering with the essay's logic

	A score of zero is given to essays which *fail to address the essay assignment.*

As you see, the guide gives the professional readers a consistent framework upon which to score each essay. Two separate readers will score each essay, independently of each other.

WHAT DO READERS EXPECT FOR THE SAT ESSAYS?

FIRST ELEMENT:

- a clearly formed opinion (point of view) on the issue with **critical thinking**, using **logical examples**, **suitable reasons**, and other **supporting evidence**

The readers expect a well-developed opinion that makes a point. Even a strong opinion may lack focus and have a vague conclusion. Have a cache (collection) of fresh and original ideas to use in your supporting evidence (for tips on this strategy, see chapter 3). These ideas will enrich the opinion or point of view of your essay. The ideas need to flow together towards a meaningful conclusion, creating a sense of completeness. Think of your favorite movie and how it ends. Well-produced movies have that sense of completeness and satisfaction. Practice fulfilling this first element in your own essays. And when you score essays, read them first for this element.

Ask yourself the following questions about the first element as you read essays for the purpose of assigning a score:

1. What is the writer's opinion on the given issue?
2. Is the opinion clear and consistent throughout the essay?
3. Does the writer support this opinion with evidence in the essay?
4. If so, how many supporting details are given as evidence?
5. Are the supporting details both relevant and engaging?
6. Does the essay have a sense of completeness to it?

For practices 1 and 2, the essays will be responding to the following writing prompt and assignment.

Writing Prompt

Rachel Carson wrote in her book Silent Spring, "The human race is challenged more than ever before to demonstrate our mastery —not over nature but of ourselves." Demonstrating mastery, in this case, refers to taking care of the environment through careful management. This includes following programs of recycling and reusing products. The challenge is to go against human desires for security and gain.

Assignment: Can people make the choice to master themselves to save nature? Plan and write an essay in which you develop your view on this issue. Support your position with reasoning and examples taken from your studies, experience, or observations.

Practice 1: Opinion and Support

Read the following short essays. Using **only** the scoring guide for opinion and support (the first element), assign each essay a score based on 6 to 0 points (with 6 being the highest score). Then write an explanation for each essay about the score you gave it. Discuss your results with classmates, your teacher, or mentor.

1 Recasting in Polymers

"There are plenty more fish in the sea." This old cliché uses fish as a metaphor to say that there are plenty more people in the world to fall in love with. Time has twisted the logic in the cliché; yes there are plenty more people, but not so many fish. Those plenty of people have been, not only eating the fish, but polluting the seas as well with over-consumption and its by-product, trash. Now it is time to make a change for balance. People have devised ways to satisfy the needs to gather and hold possessions while recycling and reusing materials, so we should master these opportunities to conserve: recycling paper, using old tires in roads, and fishing by the catch-and-release philosophy.

Philosophically speaking, security is more certain when people work together to create ways to preserve the natural environment. The paper used for this text is, hopefully, recycled—it has been reused for different purposes— and therefore trees have been saved. The road you traveled to buy this text may have had shredded tires as its base, saving space in landfills and saving petroleum products used in tire manufacturing. Fishing used to be a necessity for food; now, fishing is largely sport. The public has been encouraged to catch fish and then release them back into the water to thrive and reproduce. Some anglers resisted. They wanted to mount especially exotic sea fish. Taxidermists have devised a plan to satisfy both recyclers and anglers. They now tell people to take several pictures of the fish from different angles, release the fish and bring the pictures to have a replica of the fish made with polymer resins and then painted, mounted to display. Anglers are listening and casting their votes of approval.

As more people listen to the silence growing in the seas, they will embrace the philosophy which tells them "what comes to one—must come to us all." And when consciously choosing to recycle and reuse, mastering the desire to consume without restraint, they will feel a security which will last a lifetime—much longer than the all-you-can-eat fish buffet. Talk about over-consumption!

2 In Defense of Stuff

What is mostly green and in danger of extinction? Give up? The answer is American dollars, of course. The latest trends in recycling do harm to many of the markets they supposedly help. First they create confusion and unease for consumers. Then special recycling production drives up the costs.

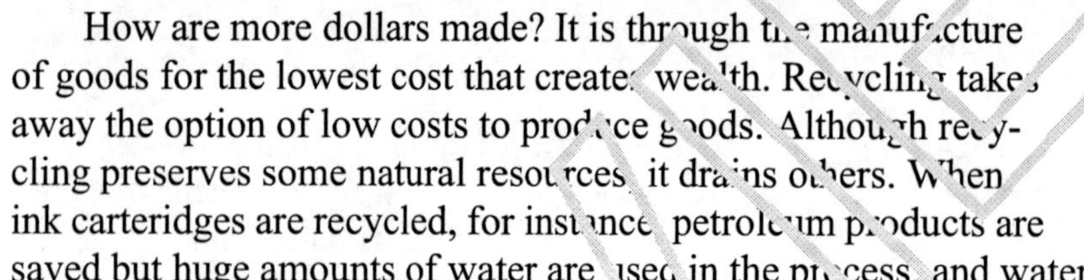

How are more dollars made? It is through the manufacture of goods for the lowest cost that creates wealth. Recycling takes away the option of low costs to produce goods. Although recycling preserves some natural resources, it drains others. When ink carteridges are recycled, for instance, petroleum products are saved but huge amounts of water are used in the process, and water is more important than chemicals. Paper is the most common product that is recycled, and the recycling process for that saves trees but takes whole rivers to finish the process so even if more trees are left there is almost no water for them to reuse to make air.

Reuse and recycling are practices which speak of uncertain, worried people. The use of plant and animal life is part of the freedom we enjoy in the America. Recycling cans is good for raising money for schools but not much else about it is good.

SECOND ELEMENT:

- effective **organization** and consistent **focus** on the opinion, as well as logically flowing **transitions** and **unity** within the essay

The **second element** allows you to make a point; this element is the organization, focus, and unity in the essay. Readers expect organization; it is the internal structure of the essay. It is both frame and glue. Strong organization begins with your stated opinion in a powerful lead and ends as you develop a memorable summary or conclusion. Your opening opinion will dictate what details you use and how you use them. Make sure your supporting details are reasonable and relevant to the stated opinion.

For all stages of the essay, you want to link each detail to a larger picture, building to the inescapable conclusion that the opinion you began with is valid. Along the way, make sure your essay follows a sequence or pattern of organization. Types of sequences are found in Chapter 1. Also use transitional words or phrases to keep the readers safely within the frame of the essay. Readers expect this type of focus and unity to keep them engaged. When you score, this will be an easy way to discover organization or find it lacking.

Ask yourself the following questions about the second element as you read essays for the purpose of assigning a score:

1. Do you understand the organizational pattern the writer is using?
2. If so, name the organization type and note if it is consistent throughout the essay.
3. Is the essay's focus consistently on the opinion?
4. Are there logical transitions which allow the essay's ideas to flow smoothly? If yes, give at least three (3) examples of transitional words or phrases.
5. Do the ideas display a unity throughout the essay? How or why not?

Practice 2: Organization and Focus for Flow and Unity

Read the following essays. Using **only** the scoring guide for organization and focus (the second element), assign each essay a score based on 6 to 0 points (with 6 being the highest score). Then write an explanation for each essay about the score you assigned it. Discuss your results with classmates, teacher, or mentor.

1 Recasting in Polymers

"There are plenty more fish in the sea." This old cliché uses fish as a metaphor to say that there are plenty more people in the world to fall in love with. Time has twisted the logic in the cliché; yes there are plenty more people, but not so many fish. Those plenty of people have been, not only eating the fish, but polluting the seas as well with over-consumption and its by-product, trash. Now it is time to make a change for balance. People have devised ways to satisfy the needs to gather and hold possessions while recycling and reusing materials, so we should master these opportunities to conserve: recycling paper, using old tires in roads, and fishing by the catch-and-release philosophy.

Philosophically speaking, security is more certain when people work together to create ways to preserve the natural environment. The paper used for this text is, hopefully, recycled — it has been reused for different purposes — and therefore trees have been saved. The road you traveled to buy this text may have had shredded tires as its base, saving space in landfills and saving petroleum products used in tire manufacturing. Fishing used to be a necessity for food; now, fishing is largely sport. The public has been encouraged to catch fish and then release them back into the water to thrive and reproduce. Some anglers resisted. They wanted to mount especially exotic sea fish. Taxidermists have devised a plan to satisfy both recyclers and anglers. They now tell people to take several pictures of the fish from different angles, release the fish and bring the pictures to have a replica of the fish, made with polymer resins and then painted, mounted to display. Anglers are listening and casting their votes of approval.

As more people listen to the silence growing in the seas, they will embrace the philosophy which tells them "what comes to one — must come to us all. And when consciously choosing to recycle and reuse, mastering the desire to consume without restraint, they will feel a sense of security which will last a lifetime — much longer than the all-you-can-eat fish buffet. Talk about over-consumption!

2 In Defense of Stuff

What is mostly green and in danger of extinction? Give up? The answer is dollars, of course. The latest trends in recycling do harm to many of the markets they supposedly help. First they create confusion and unease for consumers. Then special recycling production drives up the costs.

How are more dollars made? It is through the manufacture of goods for the lowest cost that creates wealth. Recycling takes away the option of low costs to produce goods. Although recycling preserves some natural resources, it drains others. When ink carteridges are recycled, for instance, petroleum products are saved but huge amounts of water are used in the process, and water is more important than chemicals. Paper is the most common product that is recycled, and the recycling process for that saves trees but takes whole rivers to finish the process, so even if more trees are left there is almost no water for them to reuse to make air.

Reuse and recycling are practices which speak of uncertain, worried people. The use of plant and animal life is part of the freedom we enjoy in America. Recycling cans is good for raising money for schools but not much else about it is good.

Third Element:

- displays a clear understanding of **word usage**, with **variety** and **appropriate word choice**

This **third element**, displaying a varied vocabulary, demonstrates a strong reading background and ease with language. Word choice reveals voice and adds vitality to an essay's ideas. The readers of the SAT essays expect to see thoughts written clearly and without confusion due to a word(s) used incorrectly. Incorrect word choice will make readers stop and consider the true meaning or intent of the text. When you score essays, if you find yourself stopping to question why the writer used a certain word, this is a signal that appropriate vocabulary and word choice may be lacking.

Ask yourself the following questions about the third element as you read essays for the purpose of assigning a score:

1. Scan the vocabulary used in the essay. Are any words too simple or repeated too often?
2. Scan again looking for words which are clearly misused. Has this weakened the essay's logic?
3. Are there any words which you need to think about? If so, is this because the word is unusual or used in an inappropriate way?

For practices 3 and 4, the essays will be responding to the following writing prompt and assignment.

Writing Prompt

"All changes, even the most longed for, have their melancholy, for what we leave behind us is apart of ourselves. We must die to one life before we can enter another."

Anatole France

Assignment: Does every change in a person's life make a sorrowful impression? Plan and write an essay in which you develop your point of view on this issue. Support your position with reasons and evidence brought from your studies, experience, or observations.

Practice 3: Wise Word Usage

Read the following essays. Using **only** the scoring guide for vocabulary and word choice (the third element), assign each essay a score based on 6 to 0 points (with 6 being the highest score). Then write an explanation for each essay about the score you assigned it. Discuss your results with classmates, a teacher, or mentor.

1 Changing Times

There is a saying that goes "you can't make an omlet without scrambling some eggs. You see, some of the most simple things in life take breaking. Then they can be made into something new. Like when you leave high school for a college or a tech school. That is something good but you got to get used to it. Some people seem to like the different place and people. Thus they are sad to say goodbye to some of the things they know.

Another kind of breaking goes into taking more tests. You have to crack some books to get a good grade. That may be a new thing for a lot of students. Other people seem to do ok with changes: they like new places. You may have heard that today's college kids are haveing an awful time with privacy matters. Most kids have been alone in there rooms at home. Now in college rooms they have to share space. That breaks a lot of bad habits. Hopefully for some.

Remember, change can be a good thing. Like when you go home for holidays and your family has changed a favorite restaurant. Now they go to one you prefer. And like the song says, don't worry—be happy. Change can be a good thing. For some.

2 Got Change?

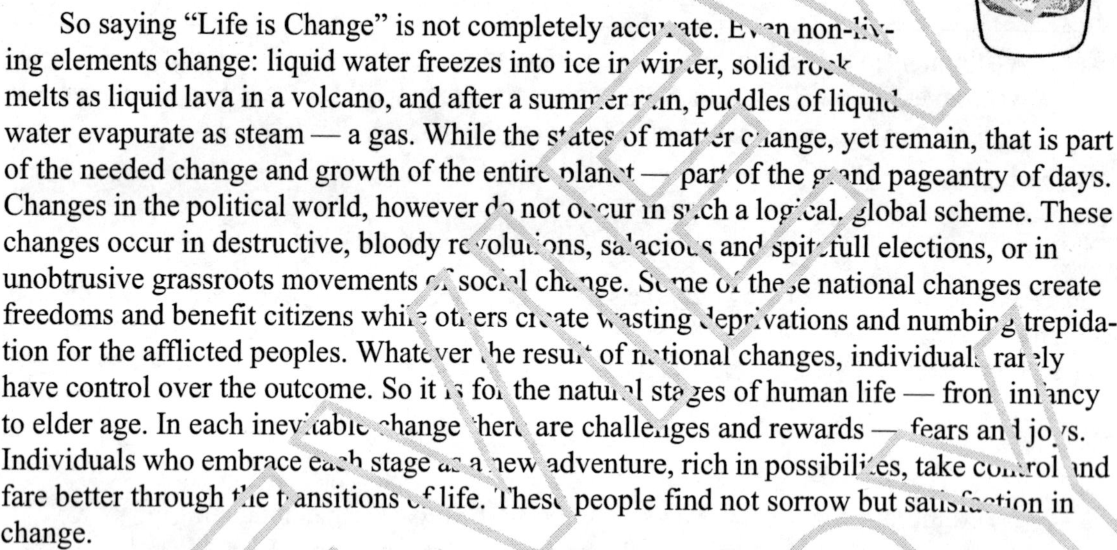

There are several definitions for "change:" to substitute, to transform, to break a dollar. All these involve some loss of properties, or substance, while gaining different ones. In the natural world, states of matter change with seasons, in the political world, nations change with human whims and in all cultures, peoples change as they live through different stages of life. To say that tap water changing to ice cubes so to cool sweet tea is a melancholy event cannot be true. Each particular change deserves more consideration.

So saying "Life is Change" is not completely accurate. Even non-living elements change: liquid water freezes into ice in winter, solid rock melts as liquid lava in a volcano, and after a summer rain, puddles of liquid water evapurate as steam — a gas. While the states of matter change, yet remain, that is part of the needed change and growth of the entire planet — part of the grand pageantry of days. Changes in the political world, however do not occur in such a logical, global scheme. These changes occur in destructive, bloody revolutions, salacious and spitefull elections, or in unobtrusive grassroots movements of social change. Some of these national changes create freedoms and benefit citizens while others create wasting deprivations and numbing trepidation for the afflicted peoples. Whatever the result of national changes, individuals rarely have control over the outcome. So it is for the natural stages of human life — from infancy to elder age. In each inevitable change there are challenges and rewards — fears and joys. Individuals who embrace each stage as a new adventure, rich in possibilities, take control and fare better through the transitions of life. These people find not sorrow but satisfaction in change.

To generalise and say that even good transitions or changes create saddness trivializes the majesty of the natural world, the force of the political world and the progression of the human life span. Just as a flexible paper dollar transforms into hard metal coins as jingling pocket change, what has been purchased is a substitute for the comfort of the paper dollar and the remaining hard, cold metal endures. Maybe declaring a national holiday would lessen fears of change — Merry Change Day! Yes, that is one holiday that would never end.

Fourth and Fifth Elements:

- a variety of **sentence structures**, adding to the essay's flow of ideas and pace
- few errors in **grammar, usage**, and **mechanics**

The **fourth** and **fifth elements** contribute to an expected positive experience for readers. Varied sentence structures and skills in writing mechanics play a vital role in communicating your thoughts clearly and gracefully. The SAT essays are written in rough draft form, but these elements are necessary for the logic and clarity of an essay. When scoring an essay, you will be able to count and label the sentence types as well as noting punctuation which should be added or deleted. Especially note if the errors interfere with the essay's logic.

Ask yourself the following questions about the fourth and fifth elements as you read essays for the purpose of assigning a score:

1. Is there a pattern of sentences used or is there a variety of sentence types?
2. What is the effect of repeated types of sentences or sentence variety on the essay?
3. Are there errors in grammar and usage in the essay? If so, describe them and their effect, if any, on the essay.
4. Does the essay have errors in mechanics? If so, describe them and their effect, if any, on the essay.

Practice 4: Sentence Structure Variety and Consistent Mechanics

Read the following essays. Using **only** the scoring guides for a variety of sentence structures and correct mechanics (the fourth and fifth elements), assign each essay a score based on 6 to 0 points (with 6 being the highest score). Then write an explanation for each essay about the score you assigned it. Discuss your results with classmates, teacher, or mentor.

1 Changing Times

There is a saying that goes "you can't make an omlet without scrambling some eggs. You see some of the most simple things in life take breaking. Then they can be made into something new. Like when you leave high school for a college or a tech school. That is something good but you got to get used to it. Some people seem to like the different place and people. Thus they are sad to say goodbye to some of the things they know.

Another kind of breaking goes into taking more tests. You have to crack some books, to get a good grade. That may be a new thing for a lot of students. Other people seem to do ok with changes: they like new places. You may have heard that today's college kids are haveing a awful time. It is with piracy matters. Most kids have been alone in there rooms at home. Now in college rooms they have to share space. That breaks a lot of bad habits. Hopefully for some.

Remember, change can be a good thing. Like when you go home for holidays and your family has changed a favorite restuarant. Now they go to one you have preference. And like the song says, don't worry—be happy. Change can be a good thing. For some.

2 Got Change?

There are several definitions for "change:" to substitute, to transform, to break a dollar. All these involve some loss of properties or substance, while gaining different ones. In the natural world, states of matter change with seasons, in the political world, nations change with human whims and in all cultures, peoples change as they live through different stages of life. To say that tap water changing to ice cubes so to cool sweet tea is a melancholy event cannot be true. Each particular change deserves more consideration.

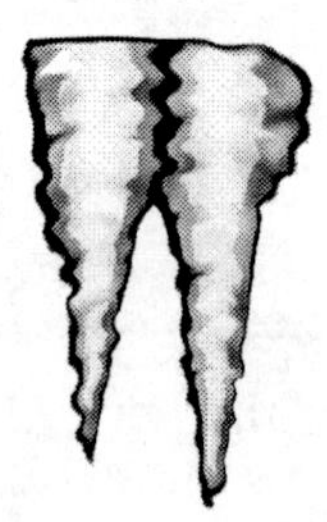

So saying "Life is Change" is not completely accurate. Even non-living elements change: liquid water freezes into ice in winter, solid rock melts as liquid lava in a volcano, and after a summer rain, puddles of liquid water evapurate as steam — a gas. While the states of matter change, yet remain, that is part of the needed change and growth of the entire planet — part of the grand pageantry of days. Changes in the political world, however do not occur in such a logical, global scheme. These changes occur in destructive, bloody revolutions, salacious and spitefull elections, or in unobtrusive grassroots movements of social change. Some of these national changes create freedoms and benefit citizens while others create wasting deprivations and numbing trepidation for the afflicted peoples. Whatever the result of national changes, individuals rarely have control over the outcome. So it is for the natural stages of human life — from infancy to elder age. In each inevitable change there are challenges and rewards — fears and joys. Individuals who embrace each stage as a new adventure, rich in possibilities, take control and fare better through the transitions of life. These people find not sorrow but satisfaction in change.

To generalise and say that even good transitions or changes create saddness trivializes the majesty of the natural world, the force of the political world and the progression of the human life span. Just as a flexible paper dollar transforms into hard metal coins as jingling pocket change, what has been purchased is a substitute for the comfort of the paper dollar and the remaining hard, cold metal endures. Maybe declaring a national holiday would lessen fears of change — Merry Change Day! Yes, that is one holiday that would never end.

How You Can Write a Successful Essay

The answer is in the scoring guide — simply write with an eye towards the elements of a successful essay. When you remember your readers' expectations, you will be on your way to a score 6 or even better. To sum up:

Write with **opinion**, close with **attitude**, and mind your **vocabulary** in the flow of ideas.

Chapter 9 Review

A. Read the following essays. Using the **complete** scoring guide for all elements of a successful essay, assign each essay a score based on 6 to 0 points (with 6 being the highest score). Then write an explanation for each essay about the score you assigned it. Discuss your results with classmates, teacher, or mentor.

To decide on a score for the complete essay, go through the questions in the chapter for each element; score each element individually; add these scores together and divide by 5 (the # of elements) and that is your **base** score. Then look at the first two elements. They are valued more by the readers so their scores count a little more. If the base score is between 4 and 5, look at the first two element scores. If they are 5 or better, score the essay as a 5. If they are scored as 4 or 3, give the whole essay a score of 4.

Writing Prompt

The science fiction writer Ursula K. LeGuin wrote a short story which explored the power which words have over human action and human thought: "Mr. Underhill answered the question: 'Because the name is the thing . . . and the true name is the true thing. To speak the name is to control the thing . . .'"
Assignment: Are names the true measure and nature of a person or a thing? Plan and write an essay in which you develop your point of view on this issue. Support your position with reasons and evidence brought from your studies, experience, or observations.

1 The Name Game

"What's in a name? A rose by any other name would smell as sweet." In this quote, William Shakespeare seems to attach less importance to names than most people. But think about it. The flower he uses in his example has a name which instantaneously brings to mind a distinct, cloying fragrance which cannot be denied. His choice of flower was deliberate in its power to transfix readers in its spell. Could any other name have worked so well?

Linnaeus thought so. He saw the whole world as a Tower of Babylon. Languages of different lands imposed different names to identical flora and fauna in the world. Linnaeus spent his life bestowing scientific names on the inhabitants of the natural world, so that the names would be universal—conferring ultimate control to *Homo sapiens*.

The names of these two men, Shakespeare and Linnaeus, have their own power. But the lives of these two people gave the names that power — the names alone are empty. In most cultures there are creation stories involving the naming of new creatures. Some traditions pair the act of creation with the act of naming — without a name, existence was not possible. But how were the names created? The English word "horse" in French is "*cheval*" in Spanish it is "*caballo*" and in Latin, the language of science, it is *Equus*. What in these names confers speed and grace and a free spirit? It is the animal which gives these qualities to the name, in any language.

This gives affirmation to anyone named Maude or Horace or Beryl or Willard. The heart and soul and drive of the person will influence the perception of the name. By the same token, the onus is on Jennifer or John or Brittany or Matthew to display positive characteristics so as to not sully their popular names. What is in a name? A name's power is to be a reflection of the true nature of the one who carries it.

2 Names. The True Story

In 1990-something, I saw a video called *Old Yeller.* My parents had tole me I could not see it — but I went to a friend's house and did anyway. My parents were right. I was bad scared, for a long time. Then I got a baby duck and named it after the movie's hero. Well the poor thing died at six months. I never, never ever should have named a pet for a dead hero. The power of naming is too frightening and forever. Was it the duck's true nature to be scarifical? Maybe. After all, ducks are often called dinner. So for all my other pets, I have chosen cute or funny names instead.

I have proof that pets, the "new-age children," do get characteristics from names. I had a Dalmatian I named Dolly. Her black and white colors fit her like a garish glove. She wasn't shy, unfortunately. After she started running with a German shepherd, she had puppies. My father called them "Damn-nations. Dolly had a nature too trusting to run free. We had to send her away — to a llama farm.

Later, I wanted a pet bird. I bought a parakeet and quickly got tired being asked what I was going to name it? I pitched a fit and yelled, "I'm naming it —Perpendicular!" Nicknamed Perp, the cornflower-blue bird chirped and chattered. Then one day someone left the door open and Perp escaped. It was like he knew Perp could also be short for "perpetrator," criminals, who like to escape. It was the power of the name that sent him flying.

A second chance, to name a parakeet came with a turquoise and ivory bird. I saw him on his perch alone in a cage and felt sorry for him. I took him home to the empty cage and named him Sinbad since his color made me think of high seas with white caps. I thought the name was cute. I forgot white caps signal a storm. Though Perp was sweet-tempered, Sinbad was mean — meaner than that. If I tried to put my hand in his cage, being friendly-like, I'd get bitten bloody. Too late I understood the double problem with his name — Sin-Bad.

Beware when naming your pets. I would look at baby books. There are a lot of them with the meanings of the names. That might stop a startling surprise. Did you hear of a Dalmatian-llama cross? The Dolly-Llama?

B. Look back to the Chapter 5 review. Use the essay you wrote for that review and assign it a score using the scoring guide found in this chapter. Then write an explanation of why you assigned the score you did.

C. Look back to the writing prompts and the assignments in this chapter. Write an essay for one of these prompts. Use all the skills you have developed through this book: the quick and messy outline, strong lead, body paragraphs, and clinching conclusion—all in 25 minutes. Walk away from the essay for a day or so. Then go back this new essay and assign it a score using this chapter's scoring guide.

SAT Writing Preparation Practice Test 1

PART I: Essay
Time—25 minutes

Writing the SAT essay will demonstrate your ability to express ideas and offer details. Use precise and concise language, choose a consistent, logical point of view, and organize your ideas in a logical progression with appropriate transitions.

On the actual SAT essay test, you will be given an answer sheet in which to write your essay, including a quick outline or plan. You will have no other paper on which to write.

For this practice essay, you will use your own paper. You may want to use this page to outline or plan, to be accustomed to the space provided for prewriting. When you write your essay, write legibly and carefully so graders may read your work.

You have twenty-five minutes to write an essay on the writing prompt below. Write a response only to this prompt, no other. Any essay that is written not addressing the prompt will receive a score of ZERO.

Read the following prompt and assignment carefully. Then consider your response.

> The fallacy of altruism, or altruistic moralism, is the sense that there is a general duty, or that morality as such requires to always, act always in the interest of others. On the other hand, an "altruistic moral aestheticism" is not a moral fallacy; for this only means that a person may act for the good of others if this seems good, which is unobjectionable as long as the action respects the autonomy of others, meaning it is not against their innocent and competent will.

Assignment: Is it always good for the good of others to help them or is it simply for the feeling of control that people act altruistically? First develop a plan and then write an essay on this topic. Choose one point of view and develop it, using examples and logical reasoning from your coursework, experience, reading, or observations.

NOTE: There is not a word count requirement for the SAT essay. However, the essay must be long enough to demonstrate your ability to organize ideas and write in a smooth progression. We recommend a minimum of 320 – 540 words.

Part II: 35 Multiple-Choice questions Improving Sentences, Identifying Sentence Errors, and Improving Paragraphs [Based on SAT Test Section 3] **Time — 35 minutes**

Directions: For each question, choose the best answer from among the five choices offered, circling the letter of your choice.

The following test items ask you to assess the correctness and effectiveness of written thought. In choosing responses, use the parameters set by standard written English in the areas of grammar, punctuation, sentence construction, and word choice.

In the sentences below, part of or the whole sentence is underlined. Beneath these sentences you will find five ways of re-phrasing the underlined part. Choice A is identical to the original; the other four responses are different. Choose the response that best expresses the meaning of the original sentence. Choose A if you think the original is correct. Choose one of the others if it is an improvement. Your choice should create the most effective sentence — clear and precise.

1. Geologists report that even though the hot springs and geysers of Yellowstone are outward signs of a huge body of magma residing just underfoot, it still does not signal an eminent eruption.
   - A. leave as is
   - B. these signs still do not signal an eminent eruption
   - C. it never signals an eminent eruption
   - D. they still does not signal an eminent eruption
   - E. an eminent eruption was still not signaled

2. In books found solace and the ideas with which she would try to aggrandize Russia.
   - A. leave as is
   - B. She would try to aggrandize Russia in books finding solace and ideas.
   - C. In books she found solace and the ideas with which she would try to aggrandize Russia.
   - D. Finding in books solace and the ideas with which she would try to aggrandize Russia.
   - E. In books her found solace and the ideas with which she would try to aggrandize Russia.

3. *Ed Wood* is a critically acclaimed film as it captures the essence of the fifties era and treating the lives of Ed Wood and Bela Lugosi with all possible humanity and compassion.

A. leave as is

B. treating the lives and as it captures the essence of the fifties era

C. as it captures the essence of the fifties era but treating the lives

D. as the essence of the fifties era it captures and treats the lives

E. as it captures the essence of the fifties era and treats the lives

4. The traditional orientation, in contrast of the revisionist one, contends that the essence of ethnic identity, meaning ethnic integrity, is simply the ability to speak one's native language.

A. leave as is

B. in contrast of its revisionist one

C. the revisionist one in contrast to

D. in contrast to the revisionist one

E. contrasting to the revisionist one

5. Greenland sharks are tolerant of copepods, tiny crustaceans, which attach to the sharks' eyes simply because the sharks live in the darkest regions of the oceans — making sight redundant.

A. leave as is

B. sharks lived in the darkest regions of the oceans

C. of a shark's life in the darkest regions of the oceans

D. of living in the oceans darkest regions

E. of living in the darkest regions of the oceans

6. As a regional chef, Mario creates unusual yet creative, sublime dishes as well as meals that also are as bland and uninspiring.

A. leave as is

B. some bland, uninspired dishes

C. bland and uninspiring meals that also

D. dishes that also let down as bland and uninspiring

E. bland and uninspired as meals

7. In Australia, the large Huntsman spiders are commonly identified by their slightly flattened bodies, colorfully banded markings, and it has odd twisted forward-splayed legs, giving it a crab-like appearance.

A. leave as is

B. it has twisted legs that splay forward oddly

C. forward-splayed odd twisted legs

D. odd twisted legs splaying forward

E. oddly twisted, forward-splayed legs

8. The Lakota's traditional language while going through revitalization, reaching more school children, and continuing to resist acquiring loan words, have not received enough government funding to be making a sustained, popular stand.

A. leave as is

B. has not received enough government funding to make

C. making government funding has not received enough

D. have not received enough government funding to be making

E. has not received government funds enough making

9. Where habitat conditions are most genial, that is where organisms will generally proliferate in stable population numbers.

   A. leave as is

   B. genial, where organisms will generally be proliferating

   C. genial, organisms will generally proliferate

   D. genial, is why organisms will generally proliferate

   E. genial, it generally is where organisms will proliferate

10. Ecological study is being conducted in the islands of the Pacific, specifically their fruit doves, bola snakes, and land snails.

    A. leve as is

    B. and specifically they are focusing on their fruit doves, bola snakes, and land snails

    C. specifically on their fruit doves, bola snakes, and land snails the intense study of their fruit doves, bola snakes, and land snails

    D. but specifically they are looking for their fruit doves, bola snakes, and land snails

11. After Harriet Tubman risked her safety leading the Underground Railroad, the Union army asked for her services as a spy and nurse in recognition of what she had already accomplished.

    A. leave as is

    B. in recognition with her already accomplishments

    C. recognizing what of what she has already accomplished

    D. to give recognition of what she had already accomplished

    E. in recognition of what she was already accomplishing

The next group of test items evaluates your skills in recognizing and correcting grammar and usage errors. There is either one error or no error in each of the test items; none of the items has more than one error. If there is an error, it is underlined and labeled with a letter: letters used are A through E. If there is an error in the test item, choose the one underlined part you would need to change to correct the test item. If there is no error and the test item is correct as is, select choice E. In choosing responses, use the parameters set by standard written English.

12. Answering (A) a request for (B) department budgets, the Juneau High School science faculty put in their (C) request for a fully developed (D) tundra ecosystem. No error (E)

13. The nature of quartz has defied (A) the logic of causality, as it (B) has produced false species more successfully through (C) crystallizing under pressure and not (D) through exposure to intense heat. No error (E)

14. Although the university's (A) writing center continued to grow, (B) it seemed that (C) Maren and Rachel were always the tutor (D) "on call." No error (E)

15. Linnaeus constructed his (A) system of naming (B) organisms according to the most familiar (C) organizing device of Western logic since (D) Aristotle, the branching system. No error (E)

16. No matter (A) how often Dr. Mathias mentored (B) our study group, we (C) seemed to have an urge of procrastinating (D) on every assignment. No error (E)

17. Poe wrote at length about the ideas him (A) kept regarding (B) the art of composition, (C) both in prose and poetry. (D) No error (E)

18. Four score (A) years after Cagle's Dairy first establish (B) a rapport with the surrounding Georgia community, the farm has been changed to (C) a child's (D) wonderland with farm tours and a corn field maze. No error (E)

19. Classical music (A) has been credited (B) with altering mental processes, including measuring (C) a substantial expansion of infant (D) IQs. No error (E)

20. DNA researchers (A) have resolved to launching (B) a public awareness program on the value (C) and infallibility (D) of DNA evidence. No error (E)

21. *Protoceratops* was almost certainly at the
A
bottom of the food chain and would
B
undoubtedly have been preyed upon by
C
almost every carnivore that stalked the
Mongolian desert, including a vicious crea-
D
ture called *Velociraptor*. No error
E

22. Performing a yearly miracle by bringing a
A B
great flood of water but fertile soil to a
C
desert, the Nile gave mankind its first great
D
civilization — Ancient Egypt. No error
E

23. Cirrus clouds are different from other
A
clouds such as cumulus and pillow clouds
B
in that they signal air direction and dry
C D
weather. No error
E

24. Bouillabaisse is good only because its
A
cooked by the French who if they cared to
B C
try could produce an excellent and nutri-
D
tious substitute out of cigar stumps and empty
matchboxes. No error
E

25. The elusive quality of the *Mona Lisa*'s smile
can be explained by the fact that it is almost
A
entirely in low spatial frequencies, and so they see it
B
best by peripheral vision. No error
C D E

26. Archeologists' writings show that even
while excavating the most revered tombs,
A
they still use King Tut's tomb as a standard
B C
more than any tomb. No error
D E

27. We have to sleep, because it is essential
A
to maintaining normal levels of cognitive
B
skills such as speech, memory, innovative
C
and flexibly thinking. No error
D E

28. We had endeavored to live so that when we
A B
come to die even the undertaker will be
C D
sorry. No error
E

29. The term "aeronautics" originated in France,
A B
but was derived from the Greek words for
C D
"air" and "to sail." No error
E

Directions: The passage below is an early draft of an essay. There are revisions which need to be made in the essay.

Read over the passage noting the flow of the paragraphs and the sense of the sentences. Then read the following questions and choose the best response for each. The questions cover several elements of the writing process: improving sentence structure or word choice; organization and point of view development. In choosing responses, use the parameters set by standard written English.

Questions 30 – 35 refer to the passage below:

(1) Do you have a best beloved place where you journey to think, to dream, and to grow in wisdom? **(2)**Since I ventured the random query. **(3)**I will offer the first answer. **(4)**My best beloved place to recharge and rehash and reaffirmed myself is the library at the refurbished city college. **(5)**At that one location I can find an overstuffed armchair, a desk with a green shaded lamp, or a longish window seat. **(6)**The atmosphere is quiet and dimmed. **(7)**And then again, if I wanted loud and bright I could go to a chain bookstore, but it is here at the library that I am my best self, more open to the moment.

(8) At the library I can access the internet for focused, quick research or I can browse shelves of books; books bound with fine-grained leather, stiffened cloth, textured cardboard, or heavy embossed paper. **(9)**I looked into learning how to re-cover books, but I was allergic to the glue. **(10)**Their pages may be yellowed, mellowed with age and use, or they may be a winter-white, a brand new hue. **(11)**The book's binding may crackle with uneasy glue when opened or it may whisper with pages turning as if in a hurry to begin the conversation between me and the text. **(12)**Some pages carry the fingerprint of previous readers, a khaki coffee ring, a darkened splat of ketchup, or a scrap of fragrant gum wrapper. **(13)**The worst souvenir I ever unearthed in a library book was a birthday card drawn and signed by a child to her father; all I could think of was her sadness at losing it or that she left it purposely in a pique of young anger.

(14) Literature often examines relationships gone awry — disabled and marred — because of lost messages.

(15) At the library my phone (including text messaging) is on silent, my headphones are stashed elsewhere, and time slows. **(16)**As well it might, since I am usually there to complete an assignment - - twenty pages of erudite writing for my Freshman Comp class! **(17)**You see, at the library I am not allowed to scream, so self-control is a given. **(18)**I hope to be a library "carrell rat" forever and I hope I have given someone the urge to take a long reaffirming moment at this best beloved place.

30. Of the following, which is the best way to revise and combine sentences 2 and 3? (reproduced below)

Since I ventured the random query. I will offer the first answer.

A. (As it is now)

B. Since I ventured the random query: I will offer the first answer.

C. Since I ventured the random query, I will offer the first answer.

D. Since I ventured the random query and will offer the first answer.

E. The random query was ventured by me, so I offer the first answer.

31. Of the following, which is the best way to revise sentence 4 (reproduced below)?

My best beloved place to recharge and rehash and reaffirmed myself is the library at the refurbished city college.

A. (As is now)

B. My best beloved place to recharge and reaffirm myself is the refurbished library at the city college.

C. My best beloved place to recharged and rehashed and reaffirmed myself is the library at the refurbished city college.

D. The library at the refurbished city college is my best beloved place to recharge and rehash and reaffirmed myself.

E. Recharging and reaffirming myself is best at my beloved place, the refurbished library at the city college.

32. In sentence 7, the phrase *And then again* is best replaced by

A. And besides that

B. As a consequence

C. Also

D. If instead I

E. By contrasting

33. Which of the following sentences should be omitted to improve the flow of the second paragraph?

A. sentence 14

B. sentence 9

C. sentence 10

D. sentence 11

E. sentence 12

34. In context, which of the following revisions to sentence 12 is most needed?

A. (As it is now)

B. Replace "the fingerprint" with "it"

C. Move "of previous readers" to after "Some pages"

D. Delete first comma

E. Add words "Such as" before "a khaki"

35. A strategy that the writer uses to unify the text is to

A. include sensory imagery

B. express disdain for chain bookstores

C. segue into short stories

D. use slang and informal language

E. keep a pessimistic tone

Part III: 14 Multiple-Choice questions **Time — 10 minutes**

More Improving Sentences [Based on SAT Test Section 10]

Directions: For each question, choose the best answer from among the five choices offered, circling the letter of your choice.

The following test items ask you to assess the correctness and effectiveness of written thought. In choosing responses, use the parameters set by standard written English in the areas of grammar, punctuation, sentence construction, and word choice.

In the sentences below, part of the sentence or the whole sentence is underlined. Beneath these sentences you will find five ways of re-phrasing the underlined part. Choice A is identical to the original; the other four responses are different. Choose the response that best expresses the meaning of the original sentence. Choose A if you think the original is correct. Choose one of the others if it is an improvement. Your choice should create the most effective sentence—clear and precise.

36. Bearded lizards from Australia are diurnal creatures because with the extremes in temperature existing in the outback region.

A. leave as is

B. with extremes for temperature existing

C. existing temperatures are extremes

D. extremes of temperature existing with

E. of the extremes in temperature existing

37. Even though F. Scott Fitzgerald lived for a time in Paris, he is considered to be the quintessential American author, revered by literary critics as well as the public.

A. leave as is

B. considered to be he is the quintessential American author, that writer revered

C. he is considered to be the quintessential American author, that writer is revered

D. he is considered to be the quintessential American author, who is revered

E. he is considered the quintessential American author and is revered

38. The two conflicting sides of the hurricane debate were that global warming is a major factor and, on the contrary, to dismiss it as an element in violent hurricane activity

A. leave as is

B. were that global warming is a major factor and that it is not

C. was that global warming was a major factor and then to dismiss it as

D. global warming were that major factor and, on the contrary, as to dismissed

E. were if global warming is a major factor and, to dismissing it as

39. The study of black holes is made possible by measuring background cosmic X-rays and looking into infrared light; both techniques are needed because the one method is different from the other in gathering collaborating evidence.

A. leave as is

B. because the two methods provide collaborating evidence.

C. because two methods are different in gathering collaborating evidence

D. the one method is different because from the other collaborating evidence

E. gathering collaborating evidence different from the other because the one method is

40. National Guard troops display athleticism, intellectualism, and patriotism as a group, after which they emerge as individuals to display how he or she is consistently remains a model citizen, even off-duty.

A. leave as is

B. how he or she are consistently

C. how they are consistently

D. how consistently he or she is

E. consistently how he or she are

41. Despite the nay saying of critics, Stephen Jay Gould's books on natural history, written with a clear, conversational voice, was often read by devoted audiences just so they could argue with him.

A. leave as is

B. by devoted audiences were often read

C. was read often by devoted audiences

D. was often devotedly read with audiences

E. were often read by devoted audiences

42. Working through emergency double shifts, the neonatal nurses finally stabilized the seven newest infants at the center.

A. leave as is

B. Working through emergencies double shifts

C. Through emergency working double shifts

D. Works through emergency double shifts

E. Emergency work through double shifts

43. Successful computer programmers do not directly compete with each other, everything in this capitalist society is a battle for the step up.

A. leave as is

B. each other, yet everything

C. each other, and everything

D. each other since everything

E. each other with everything

44. One instance of writer's block may apply to Harper Lee, who though having written a best-selling novel, did not attempt to write another greater than the first.

A. leave as is

B. another greater than the first one

C. another greater than the first bestseller book

D. yet another greater than the first greater one

E. and another greater than the first

45. Debating the pros and cons of the internet is almost hopeless, in part because of its expanding threats yet mostly because of it rapidly changing.

A. leave as is

B. changing it is rapidly

C. of how it rapidly changes

D. how rapidly it changes

E. how rapidly which changing it

46. The Federal Emergency Management Association, FEMA, cannot hardly ever say it will be completely accurate in its response predictions.

A. leave as is

B. FEMA, can hardly ever say it would be completely accurate

C. FEMA, cannot say it will be completely accurate

D. FEMA, cannot ever say it will not be completely accurate

E. FEMA, cannot be completely accurate hardly ever

47. Several species of migratory birds favored coffee bushes because of allegedly supplying an energy boost for long flights.

A. because of allegedly supplying an energy boost

B. and allegedly supplied an energy boost

C. for it was alleged to supplying an energy boost

D. because of allegedly supplying an energy boost

E. because it was alleged to supply an energy boost

48. Researchers think that dingoes fear being hunted by humans which results in their watching their packs more closely for tension and even cannibalism among the creatures.

A. leave as is

B. humans and results in their watching

C. humans but they watching results

D. humans; watching as a result they

E. humans, which results in their watching

49. The band members rising from their chairs to a glorious version of the *National Anthem.*

A. leave as is

B. Band members rising up from all their chairs to a glorious version of the *National Anthem*

C. The band members rose from their chairs to play a glorious version of the *National Anthem*

D. The band members rose from its chairs to a glorious version of the *National Anthem*

E. The band rose from his or her chairs with a glorious version of the *National Anthem*

SAT Writing Preparation Practice Test 2

PART I: Essay
Time — 25 minutes

Writing the SAT essay will demonstrate your ability to express ideas and offer details. Use precise and concise language, choose a consistent, logical point of view, and organize your ideas in a logical progression with appropriate transitions.

On the actual SAT essay test, you will be given an answer sheet in which to write your essay, including a quick outline or plan. You will have no other paper on which to write.

For this practice essay, you will use your own paper. You may want to use this page to outline or plan, to be accustomed to the space provided for prewriting. When you write your essay, write legibly and carefully, so graders may read your work.

You have twenty-five minutes to write an essay on the writing prompt below. Write a response only to this prompt, no other. Any essay that is written not addressing the prompt will receive a score of ZERO.

Read the following prompt and assignment carefully. Then consider your response to them

> *It is war that is the motor of institutions and of order: peace, right down to the smallest of its cogs, obscurely engages in war. In other words, we must decypher [make sense of] war in peace: war is the very cypher [symbol] of peace. Thus we are at war with each other; a battle front runs through our entire society, continuously and permanently, and it is this battle front which places each of us in one camp or another. There is no neutral subject; we are of necessity someone's adversary.*
>
> Excerpt from Michel Foucault, (1997)
> *"Il faut défendre la société. Cours au Collège de France. 1976*
> (Paris: coll. Hautes Etudes, Gallimard Seuil), pp. 43 – 44.

Assignment: Are elements of war found in the mechanics of peace? First develop a plan and then write an essay on this topic. Choose one point of view and develop it, using examples and logical reasoning from your coursework, experience, reading, or observations.

NOTE: There is not a word count requirement for the SAT essay. However, the essay must be long enough to demonstrate your ability to organize ideas and write in a smooth progression. We recommend a minimum of 320 – 520 words.

Part II: 35 Multiple-Choice questions

Improving Sentences, Identifying Sentence Errors, and Improving Paragraphs [Based on SAT Test Section 3]

Time — 35 minutes

Directions: For each question, choose the best answer from among the five choices offered, circling the letter of your choice.

The following test items ask you to assess the correctness and effectiveness of written thought. In choosing responses, use the parameters set by standard written English in the areas of grammar, punctuation, sentence construction, and word choice.

In the sentences below, part of or the whole sentence is underlined. Beneath these sentences you will find five ways of re-phrasing the underlined part. Choice A is identical to the original; the other four responses are different. Choose the response that best expresses the meaning of the original sentence. Choose A if you think the original is correct. Choose one of the others if it is an improvement. Your choice should create the most effective sentence — clear and precise.

1. During the nineteenth century, the Ottoman government was able to extend its influence from the center to the periphery partly because of its great wealth and because of it assigning regional governors to control its subjects.

A. leave as is
B. it assigns regional governors
C. assigning it has regional governors
D. it assigns of regional governors
E. of the assignment of regional governors

2. Vladimir Nabokov was a noted taxidermist who divided and meticulously described species of butterflies, but lacking the blind ambition to unify or generalize.

A. leave as is
B. While Vladimir Nabokov was a noted taxidermist who divided and meticulously described species of butterflies, he lacked
C. Because he was a noted taxidermist who divided and meticulously described species of butterflies, but Vladimir Nabokov was lacking
D. While Vladimir Nabokov was a noted taxidermist who divided and meticulously described species of butterflies but lacked
E. Even though, he was a noted taxidermist who divided and meticulously described species of butterflies, Vladimir Nabokov lacking

3. Any juggler knows that the real crowd pleaser is not the hardest task, which causes jugglers scheduling feats that would maim if any error were allowed.
   A. leave as is
   B. task, but rather scheduling jugglers causes
   C. task but jugglers scheduling
   D. task; as such, jugglers schedule
   E. task, for which causes scheduling of jugglers

4. After wasting years waiting for genius to strike, Stendhal finally settled on a regimen, everyday he wrote "twenty lines a day — genius or not."
   A. regimen, everyday he
   B. regimen, for everyday he
   C. regimen because of everyday he
   D. regimen: further everyday he
   E. regimen even everyday he

5. We refer to the 1918 outbreak of flu as the greatest pandemic in recorded history, because it took at least 21 million lives in just two years.
   A. leave as is
   B. just because of it taking at least
   C. because, it took at least
   D. for because it took at least
   E. because of taking at least

6. In the 1960s, mnemonic devices created using natural strategies for memorization was included and studied as a learning tool in scientific discussion for the first time.
   A. leave as is
   B. as a learning tool was included and studied
   C. being learning tools included and studied were
   D. was as a learning tool, included and studied
   E. were included and studied as learning tools

7. Speechmaking in the eighteenth century for political candidates with its poor lighting, lack of cue cards, and few comfortable venues, testing even Lincoln's presenting the two-minute Gettysburg Address.
   A. leave as is
   B. venues a test even of Lincoln's presenting
   C. venues tested even Lincoln's presentation of
   D. venues, was testing of even Lincoln's presenting
   E. venues test even Lincoln's presentation

8. Emerson once opined about the wasted talents of his friend Thoreau, but in acknowledging his stature in literary circles, he was right to lead people out picking huckleberries rather than writing learned philosophies.
   A. leave as is
   B. and acknowledging his stature in literary circles, it proves that he was right
   C. an acknowledgement of his stature in literary circles proves that he was right
   D. acknowledging his literary stature, he was proved right
   E. an acknowledgement being made about his stature in literary circles proved he was right

9. To work with the government, one needs to note the worth of its officials, their dedication to the letter of the law and the way he or she handles obstreperous citizens.
   A. leave as is
   B. the way they handle
   C. the way to handle
   D. the way they handles
   E. the way their handling

10. As the only food that never spoils, the use of honey has leaped even as production has slowed, naturally driving the cost of a jar up to record levels.

A. leave as is

B. naturally this drove the cost of a jar up to record levels

C. naturally, it caused driving the cost of a jar up to record levels

D. but the natural drive of the cost of a jar up to record levels

E. therefore naturally it drives the cost of a jar up to record levels

11. Scientists believe that the reason hurricane Katrina was so destructive while Rita was not is that the winds and surge strength of Katrina was far greater than Rita's.

A. leave as is

B. that much greater than was Rita's

C. greater by far in strength than Rita's

D. far greater than that of Rita's winds and surge strength

E. far greater winds and storm surge than that of Rita's

The next group of test items evaluates your skills in recognizing and correcting grammar and usage errors. There is either one error or no error in each of the test items; none of the items has more than one error. If there is an error, it is underlined and labeled with a letter: letters used are A through E. If there is an error in the test item, choose the one underlined part you would need to change to correct the test item. If there is no error and the test item is correct as is, select choice E. In choosing responses, use the parameters set by standard written English.

12. If a survey were taken of small tropical port
A
towns for levels of unity and integration,
B
Colonia would rate certain in the mid-range.
C D
No error
E

13. Looking out at the universe, they are looking
A B
back in time, because light had to leave dis-
C
tant objects a long time ago, to reach us now.
D
No error
E

14. In her book *Annie John,* Jamaica Kincaid has
A
decided creating a classic bildungsroman or
B
growing-up novel, which chronicles the
C
moral, psychological, and intellectual development of a character. No error
D E

15. The Election Day contest was bitter, and to the last vote scintillating, but principles triumphs
A B C
over party chicanery, and we won all but the Tax
D
Collector. No error
E

16. Reasonable orders are easy enough to obey; therefore, capricious, bureaucratic or plain
A (to obey; therefore) B (or)
idiotic demands seem to form the
C (to form)
majority of disciplines. No error
D (majority of disciplines.) E (No error)

17. The unrecorded past is none other than our
A (none other than)
old friend, the tree in the primeval forest
B (in) C (primeval)
which fell slow without being heard.
D (slow)
No error
E

18. When a red-headed person is above a certain
A (When) B (above)
level of social grade, their hair is considered
C (level of social) D (their)
to be auburn. No error
E

19. Again and again, public opinion surveys
A (surveys)
over the last decade have shown that people
B (have shown) C (that)
want the government to remedy eco-
D (to remedy)
nomic injustice. No error
E

20. Ethiopia's Derartu Tulu blew away her rivals
A (Ethiopia's)
to win the women's elite race from her com-
B (to win) C (women's) D (her)
patriot Worknesh Kidane. No error
E

21. Whale lice spend their entire lives clinging to right whales, but both of these species
A (whales, but) B (of these species)
share a common ecological history. No error
C (share) D (ecological) E (No error)

22. When a person runs, the body makes sure
A (When a person runs) B (body)
the muscles cope by keeping it supplied with
C (it)
oxygen to help burn fuel to make the energy
D (to help burn)
they need. No error
E

23. While law is part of society, the academic
A (While)
study of law, neither as a science, that is,
B (neither)
jurisprudence, and by students preparing to
C (preparing)
be lawyers is taught at specialized law schools.
D (schools)
No error
E

24. Sachi voted in the student council election
A (in)
before her met friends on the way to work at
B (her) C (on the way) D (at)
the community center pool. No error
E

25. Arthur Wynne based his new game, called a
A (his) B (called)
crossword puzzle, to a similar but much older
C (to)
game (played in ancient Pompeii) called Magic
Squares or word square. No error
D (or) E (No error)

26. Figi resembles India in its establishment of a
A (resembles) B (its)
Democratic government, but unlike
C (government, but)
its politicians, Figi is lead by a majority of foreign-
D (its politicians)
ers. No error
E

27. Easter Island has received much attention for
A
its mysterious, giant statues called *moai*,
B
which some critics denounce to be manufactured
C
in this century. No error
D E

28. The first book on tea "Ch'a Ching,"
A B
comprising three volumes circa 780 AD,
C
were written by the Chinese author Lu Yu.
D
No error
E

29. Its a matter of common experience that
A B
things get more disordered and chaotic with
C D
time. No error
E

Directions: The passage below is an early draft of an essay. There are revisions which need to be made in the essay.

Read over the passage noting the flow of the paragraphs and the sense of the sentences. Then read the following questions and choose the best response for each. The questions cover several elements of the writing process: improving sentence structure or word choice; organization and point of view development. In choosing responses, use the parameters set by standard written English.

Questions 30 – 35 refer to the passage below:

(1) College bound and bound into knots trying to make decisions about the best college. **(2)**That is what I have been experiencing in the past semester. **(3)**There is the location to consider; the type of coursework being sought; the living quarter's livability; and the most pressing issue, the amount of financial aid available. **(4)**I would still be trapped perusing virtual tours on the internet if I were not rescued by the advice and assistance of my counselor, Ms. Roberts.

(5) All counselors carry the burdens of parent/teacher meetings and student venting sessions. **(6)**On the other hand, Ms. Roberts has taken it on herself to find just the right query to help a student target in on the most appropriate choices for college. **(7)**She has developed a survey sheet that breaks the ice for the indecisive student. **(8)**This survey may be completed independently or in peer groups. **(9)**Parents are involved as well. **(10)**On the surveys, there are interview questions for parents to be administered by their fledgling college-bound students. **(11)**When a student has narrowed choices down to two or three, Ms. Roberts shepherds a group with the same college choices on a field trip to said colleges. **(12)**Taking the campus by storm, *en masse*, gives the visiting students a sense of control in the process. **(13)**It is the lure of these field trips that keeps students on target to unbind themselves and choose.

(14) In an unforeseen shift, my counselor Ms. Roberts will be leaving for a different type of college herself next year. **(15)**It is the college of the world; she is joining a new "Teacher's without Borders" group — like the doctors everyone has heard of. **(16)**She will be traveling for two years with this program teaching English in Japan, the Czech Republic and in China. **(17)**She is bound for parts unknown to us but where she goes she will set minds free, just as she did on behalf of her befuddled students.

30. Of the following, which is the best way to revise and combine sentences 1 and 2? (reproduced below)

College bound and bound into knots trying to make decisions about the best college. That is what I have been experiencing in the past semester.

A. leave as is

B. College bound and bound into knots trying to make decisions about the best college; I have been experiencing all this in the past semester.

C. Even though college bound and bound into knots trying to make decisions about the best college, I have been experiencing this in the past semester.

D. College bound and bound into knots trying to make decisions about the best college: I have been experiencing this in the past semester.

E. College bound and bound into knots trying to make decisions about the best college and that is what I have been experiencing in the past semester.

31. Of the following, which is the best way to revise sentence 4 (reproduced below)?

I would still be trapped perusing virtual tours on the internet if I were not rescued by the advice and assistance of my counselor Ms. Roberts.

A. leave as is

B. Ms. Roberts rescued me with advice and assistance or I would still be trapped perusing virtual tours on the internet.

C. Because I would still be trapped perusing virtual tours on the internet, I was rescued by the advice and assistance of my counselor, Ms. Roberts.

D. I would still be trapped perusing virtual tours on the internet if Ms. Roberts my counselor had not been rescuing me with advice and assistance.

E. I would still be trapped perusing virtual tours on the internet were it not for the advice and assistance of my counselor, Ms. Roberts.

32. In sentence 6, the phrase *On the other hand* is best replaced by

A. And anyway

B. As a consequence

C. But

D. Also

E. Then again

33. Which of the following sentences should be omitted to improve the flow of the second paragraph?

A. None

B. Sentence 8

C. Sentence 9

D. Sentence 10

E. Sentence 11

34. In context, which of the following is the best way to phrase the underlined portion of sentence 12? (reproduced below)

<u>In an unforeseen shift</u>, my counselor Ms. Roberts will be leaving for a different type of college herself next year.

A. (As it is now)

B. Even more helpful

C. Ever since

D. As a natural consequence

E. Heedlessly

35. A strategy that the writer uses within the third paragraph is to

A. include sensory imagery.

B. express disdain for the counselor's choice.

C. make false assumptions and exaggerations.

D. use a lofty, elevated tone as tribute.

E. take elements of propaganda to enlist others.

Part III: 14 Multiple-Choice questions

Time—10 minutes

More Improving Sentences [Based on SAT Test Section 10]

Directions: For each question, choose the best answer from among the five choices offered, circling the letter of your choice.

The following test items ask you to assess the correctness and effectiveness of written thought. In choosing responses, use the parameters set by standard written English in the areas of grammar, punctuation, sentence construction, and word choice.

In the sentences below, part of or the whole sentence is underlined. Beneath these sentences you will find five ways of re-phrasing the underlined part. Choice A is identical to the original; the other four responses are different. Choose the response that best expresses the meaning of the original sentence. Choose A if you think the original is correct. Choose one of the others if it is an improvement. Your choice should create the most effective sentence — clear and precise.

36. Rockets from the historical records of Chinese scientists, which are faithfully described in the NASA Web site.

A. leave as is

B. Rockets from the historical records of Chinese scientists, which are faithfully described in the NASA Web site, operated similarly to bottle rockets.

C. Rockets from the historical records of Chinese scientists that are faithfully described in the NASA Web site.

D. Operating similar to bottle rockets, rockets from the historical records of Chinese scientists, which are faithfully described in the NASA Web site.

E. Rockets from the historical records of Chinese scientists operating similarly to bottle rockets, which are faithfully described in the NASA Web site

37. Ethnic cuisines allow variety for every appetite, since there are a world of different spices and foodstuffs at most neighborhood markets.

A. every appetite, since there are

B. each appetites, since there are

C. satisfying every appetite, since there are

D. every appetite since there are

E. every appetite since there is

38. From the moment primitive humans fashioned the first mask, the issues of taking on someone else's identity will be a source of fascination and a theme for horror and detective literature, provoking doubts about the first facial transplant.

A. leave as is

B. identity was a source

C. source of identity will be

D. identities will be a source

E. identity, will be sources

39. Scientists report finding newly birthed black holes, barely seconds old, in a confused state of <u>existence who begin pulling in</u> and pushing away intergalactic matter.

A. leave as is
B. beginning existence who pulling in
C. existence that begin pulling in
D. that existence who are pulling
E. whose existence they begin pull

40. Vegetarians are those people who eat alternative foods eschewing animal products, <u>including meat, fish, fowl, and sometimes dairy products</u>.

A. leave as is
B. that include meat, fish, fowl, and sometimes dairy products
C. including meat, fish, fowl, but sometimes dairy products
D. sometimes meat, fish, fowl, and dairy products
E. meat, fish, fowl, including and dairy products

41. Unable to accept that Amelia Earhart had simply disappeared and perished, some people believed spy planes of an unfriendly nation attack <u>about her mishap</u> in the ocean.

A. leave as is
B. about their mishaps
C. by causing her mishap
D. for her mishap
E. from her to be mishap

42. One of the original 13 colonies before the Revolutionary War, Connecticut established a reputation for legislative action, <u>besides being known as the "Constitution State."</u>

A. leave as is
B. for besides being known the "Constitution State."
C. being known besides as the "Constitution State."
D. besides being known for the "Constitution State."
E. partly by being known as the "Constitution State."

43. Where the Rocky Mountains form the Continental <u>Divide, this is where the mountainous ridge running north to south along North America causes</u> water to drain to different sides of the continent.

A. leave as is
B. Divide, the mountainous ridge running north to south along North America causes
C. Divide, this is where the mountainous ridge that runs north to south along North America causes
D. Divide, where the mountainous ridge running north to south along North America causes
E. Divide, the mountainous ridge this is where running north to south along North America causes

44. President Franklin D. Roosevelt set up many new projects and agencies to help the hardest hit areas during the Great Depression <u>since many people were out of work</u>, burdening the economy.

A. leave as is
B. there were since many people out of work
C. because of there were too many people out of work
D. since out of work people were too many
E. since there were too many people out working

45. In a humorous tone, radio host George Hay announced that the <u>audience had been listening to classic opera, but from then on he would present them with</u> "The Grand Ole Opry."

A. leave as is

B. audiences listening to classic opera, but from then on he would present them with

C. audience had been listening to classic opera, but from then on he would present

D. listening to classic opera the audience had been, and from then on he would present with

E. had audiences been listening to classic opera, but from then on he would present them with

46. On May 17, 1875, the horse, Aristides, a Thoroughbred named after an ancient Greek general, crossed the finish line, <u>flying ahead of the field himself in first place</u> won the first ever Kentucky Derby.

A. leave as is

B. flying ahead of himself in the field of first place

C. flying ahead of the field in first place

D. ahead of the flying field himself in first place

E. himself in first place, flying ahead of the field

47. Even when Annie John, in the Jamaica Kincaid novel of the same name, rebels against her mother and teachers, her emerging personality <u>takes strength, which derives from her</u> innate abilities and insolence.

A. leave as is

B. derived strength, taken from her

C. taking strength, which derives from her

D. takes strength, derived from her

E. takes strength, which derives from she

48. Wearing headphones that fit in the ear canal, mowing the grass without ear plugs, and riding a motorcycle without a helmet <u>have all been proven to be causing</u> hearing loss in all age groups and all cultural backgrounds.

A. leave as is

B. have all been proven causing

C. has all been proven causing to be

D. having all been proven to cause

E. have all proven to cause

49. Launching a plan for non-violent protest, <u>activists in Albany, Georgia began boycotts and sit-ins at local restaurants and department stores, but failed to spark national news since Albany police treated the activists with civility</u>.

A. leave as is

B. in Albany, Georgia activists began boycotts and sit-ins at local restaurants and department stores, but failed to spark national news since Albany police treated the activists with civility

C. boycotts and sit-ins began by activists in Albany, Georgia at local restaurants and department stores, failed to spark national news since Albany police treated activists civilly

D. activists in Albany, Georgia began boycotting and sitting-ins at local restaurants and department stores, so failed to spark national news since Albany police treated the activists with civility

E. activists failing to spark national news in Albany, Georgia had began boycotts and sit-ins at local restaurants and department stores, and Albany police treated the activists with civility